MOTHER,
COME HOME

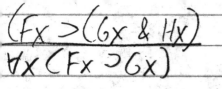

$(Fx \supset (Gx \ \& \ Hx)$

$\forall x (Fx \supset Gx)$

STEP

$\forall x$ .....

$\ddot{} \ a \ \ddot{}$

$\sim \ddot{a} \sim$

$\forall x \sim x$

$\forall x (Fx \supset (Gx \ \& \ Hx))$

$Fa \supset Ga \ \& \ Ha$

(1)

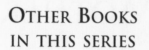

$x Fx \ \lor$

$\exists x (F$

$\exists x \ Fx$

$\vdots$

$\exists x (Fx \ \lor$

$\exists x ($

$\overline{P}^{(i)} \quad \overline{G}$

$\dot{R}$

R

ANY —

Other Books
in this Series

JUST OFF TRANSPARENT

THE NEW GLASSES

THE PAPER HIDE

$\exists x (Gx) \quad \exists Gx \quad \exists x$ (3) (2)

$\exists x (F$

$x)$

me and a

If Mary loves anyone, then she loves John

$(\exists x Lmx) \supset Lmj$ OR $\forall x (Lmx \supset Lmj)$

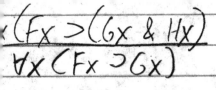

Mother,
Come Home

Paul Hornschemeier

With An Introduction By
Thomas Tennant

DARK HORSE BOOKS

DIANA SCHUTZ
collection editor

PAUL HORNSCHEMEIER
designer

MIKE RICHARDSON
publisher

This volume collects new material along with issues 2-4 of the comic
book series *Forlorn Funnies*, originally published by Absence of Ink.

Published by
Dark Horse Books
A division of Dark Horse Comics, Inc.
10956 SE Main Street
Milwaukie, Oregon 97222

First edition: November 2003
ISBN 1-59307-037-3

3 5 7 9 10 8 6 4 2
Printed in China

FOR MY FATHER.
WITH GREATER RESPECT EACH DAY.

MOTHER,
COME HOME

INTRODUCTION
TO THE SECOND EDITION

SECTION ONE:
"OUR MUTUAL DISAPPEARANCE"

INTRODUCTION BY THOMAS TENNANT

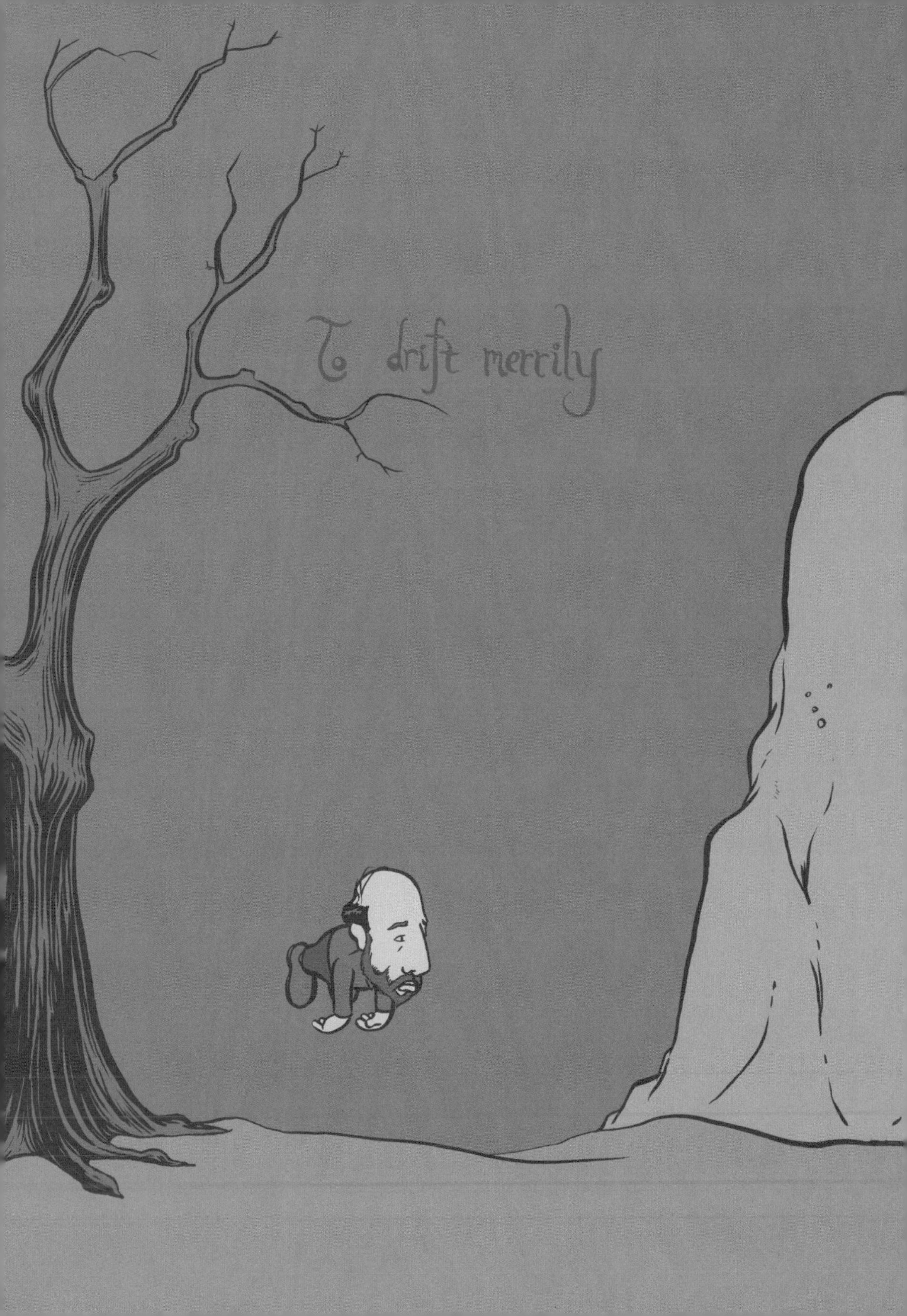
To drift merrily

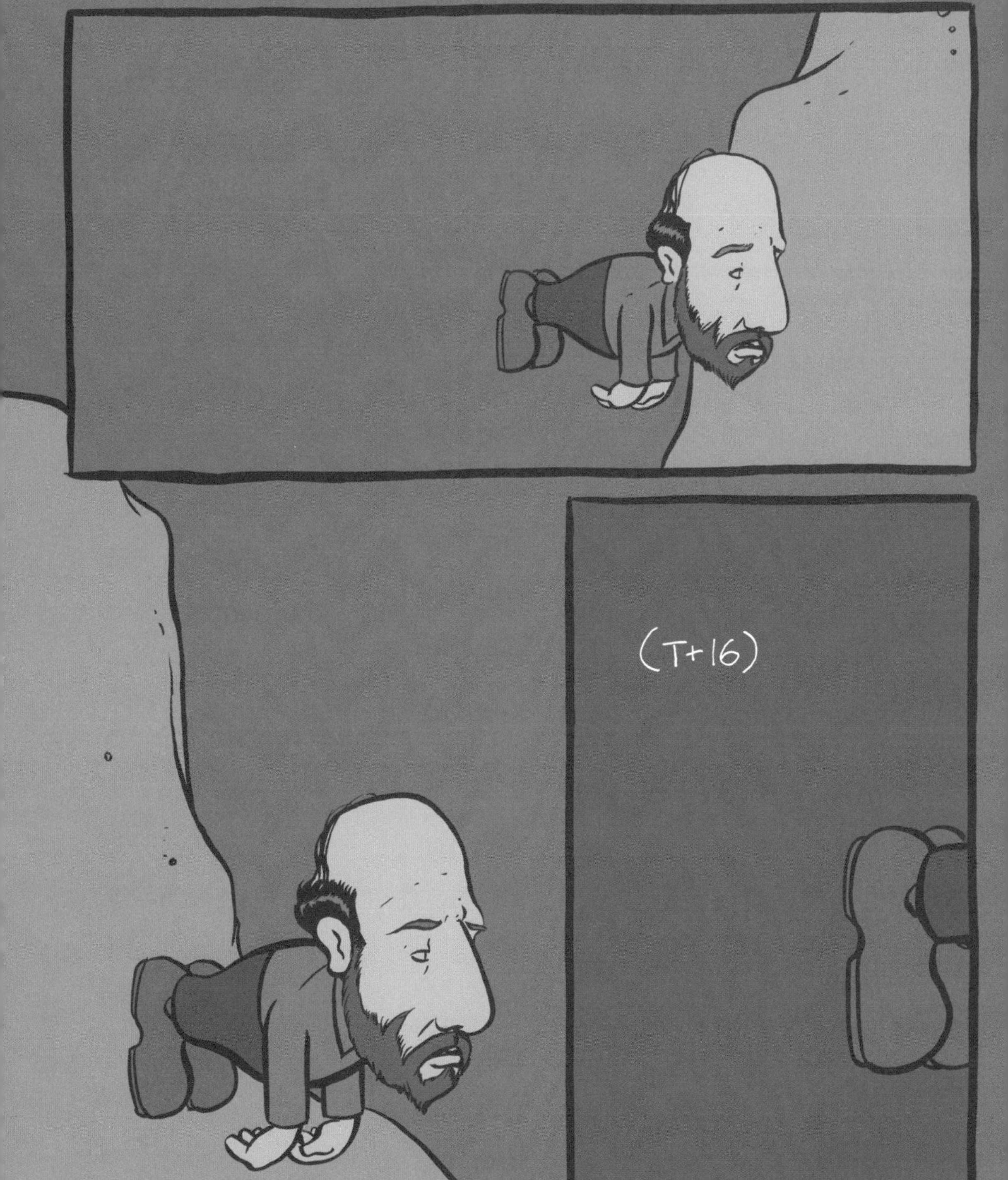
(T+16)

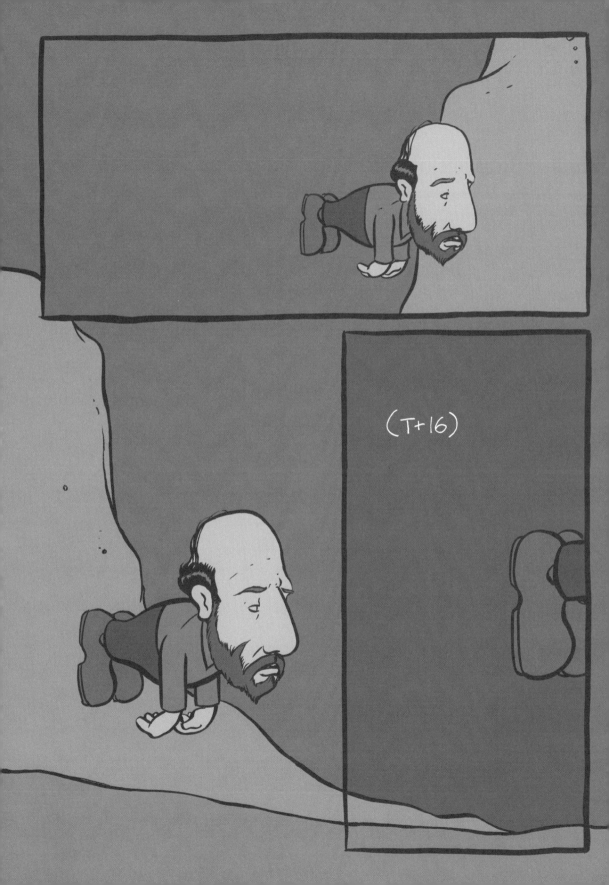

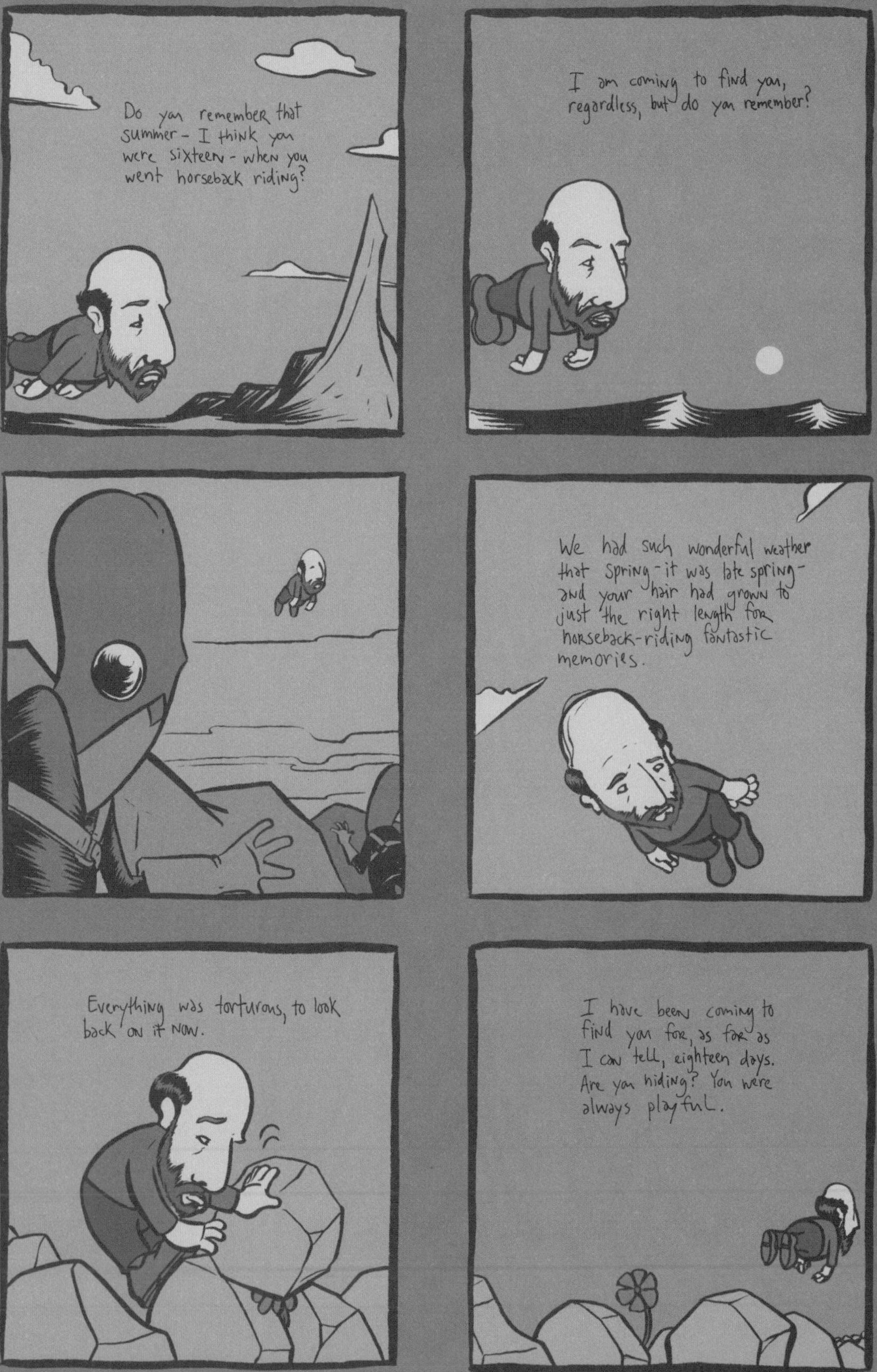
Do you remember that summer - I think you were sixteen - when you went horseback riding?
I am coming to find you, regardless, but do you remember?
We had such wonderful weather that Spring - it was late spring - and your hair had grown to just the right length for horseback-riding fantastic memories.
Everything was torturous, to look back on it now.
I have been coming to find you for, as far as I can tell, eighteen days. Are you hiding? You were always playful.

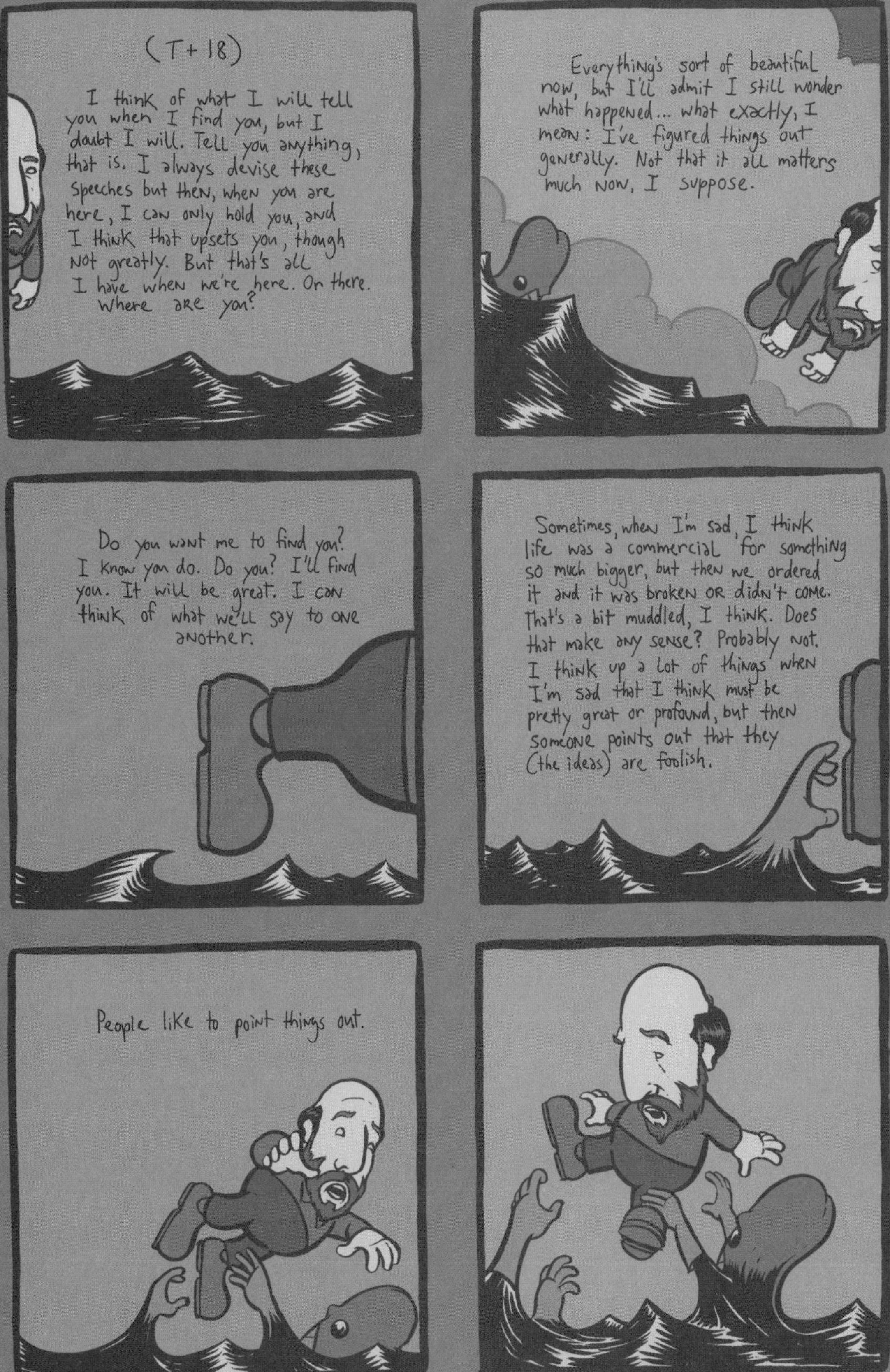
(T+18)
I think of what I will tell you when I find you, but I doubt I will. Tell you anything, that is. I always devise these speeches but then, when you are here, I can only hold you, and I think that upsets you, though not greatly. But that's all I have when we're here. Or there. Where are you?
Everything's sort of beautiful now, but I'll admit I still wonder what happened... what exactly, I mean: I've figured things out generally. Not that it all matters much now, I suppose.
Do you want me to find you? I know you do. Do you? I'll find you. It will be great. I can think of what we'll say to one another.
Sometimes, when I'm sad, I think life was a commercial for something so much bigger, but then we ordered it and it was broken or didn't come. That's a bit muddled, I think. Does that make any sense? Probably not. I think up a lot of things when I'm sad that I think must be pretty great or profound, but then someone points out that they (the ideas) are foolish.
People like to point things out.

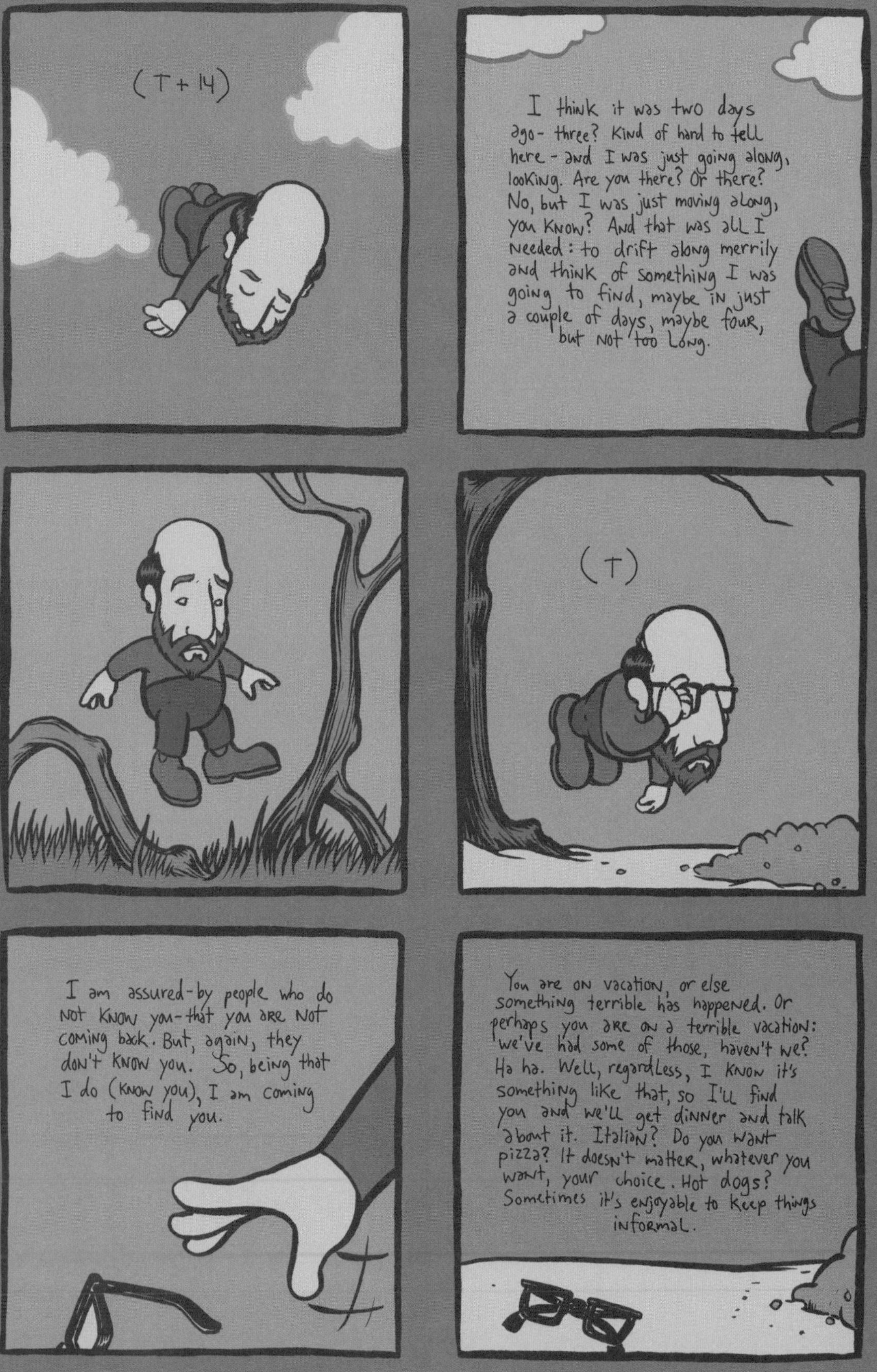
(T + 14)
I think it was two days ago - three? Kind of hard to tell here - and I was just going along, looking. Are you there? Or there? No, but I was just moving along, you know? And that was all I needed: to drift along merrily and think of something I was going to find, maybe in just a couple of days, maybe four, but not too long.
(T)
I am assured - by people who do not know you - that you are not coming back. But, again, they don't know you. So, being that I do (know you), I am coming to find you.
You are on vacation, or else something terrible has happened. Or perhaps you are on a terrible vacation: we've had some of those, haven't we? Ha ha. Well, regardless, I know it's something like that, so I'll find you and we'll get dinner and talk about it. Italian? Do you want pizza? It doesn't matter, whatever you want, your choice. Hot dogs? Sometimes it's enjoyable to keep things informal.

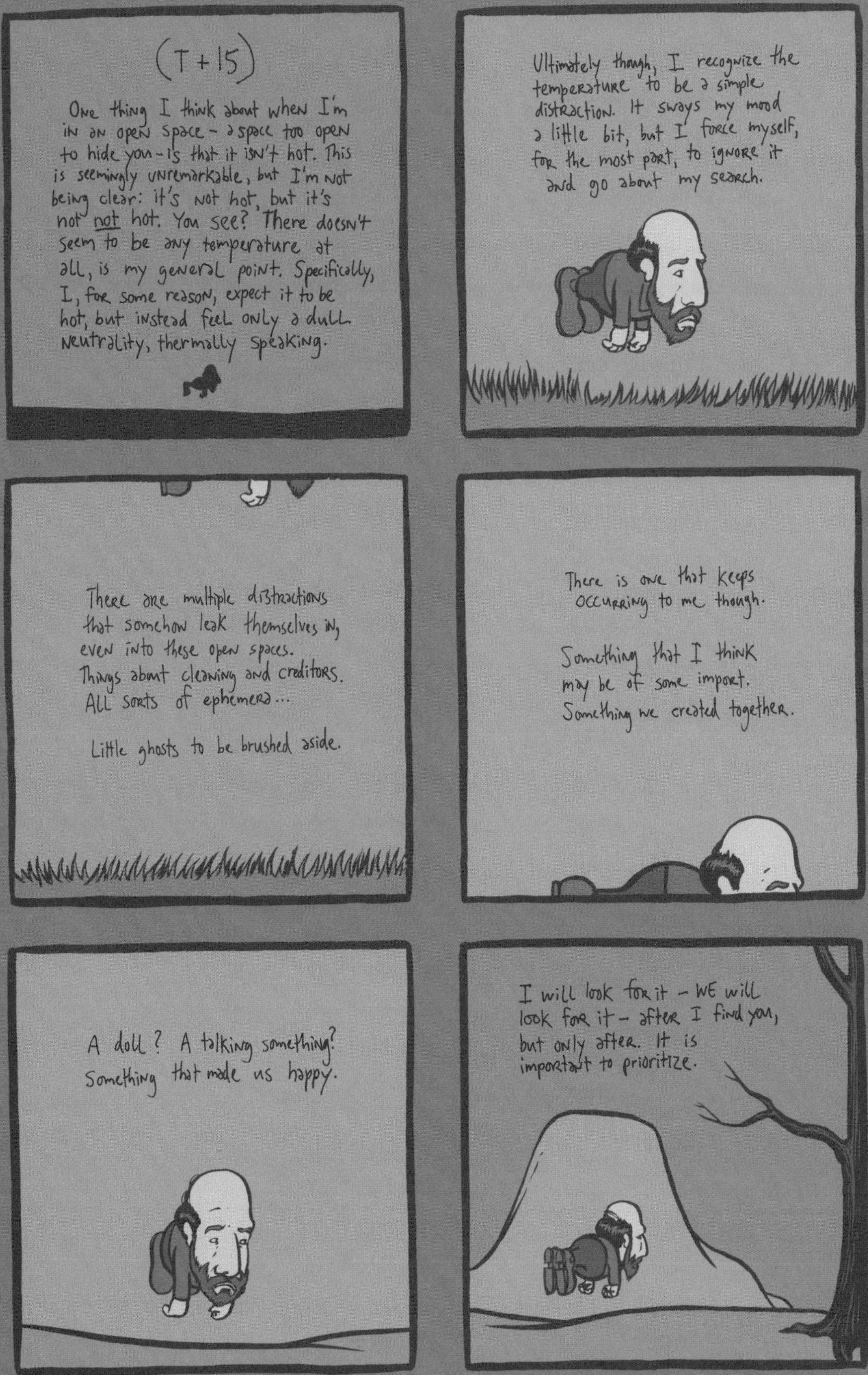
(T+15)
One thing I think about when I'm in an open space - a space too open to hide you - is that it isn't hot. This is seemingly unremarkable, but I'm not being clear: it's not hot, but it's not not hot. You see? There doesn't seem to be any temperature at all, is my general point. Specifically, I, for some reason, expect it to be hot, but instead feel only a dull neutrality, thermally speaking.
Ultimately though, I recognize the temperature to be a simple distraction. It sways my mood a little bit, but I force myself, for the most part, to ignore it and go about my search.
There are multiple distractions that somehow leak themselves in, even into these open spaces. Things about cleaning and creditors. All sorts of ephemera...
Little ghosts to be brushed aside.
There is one that keeps occurring to me though.
Something that I think may be of some import. Something we created together.
A doll? A talking something? Something that made us happy.
I will look for it - WE will look for it - after I find you, but only after. It is important to prioritize.

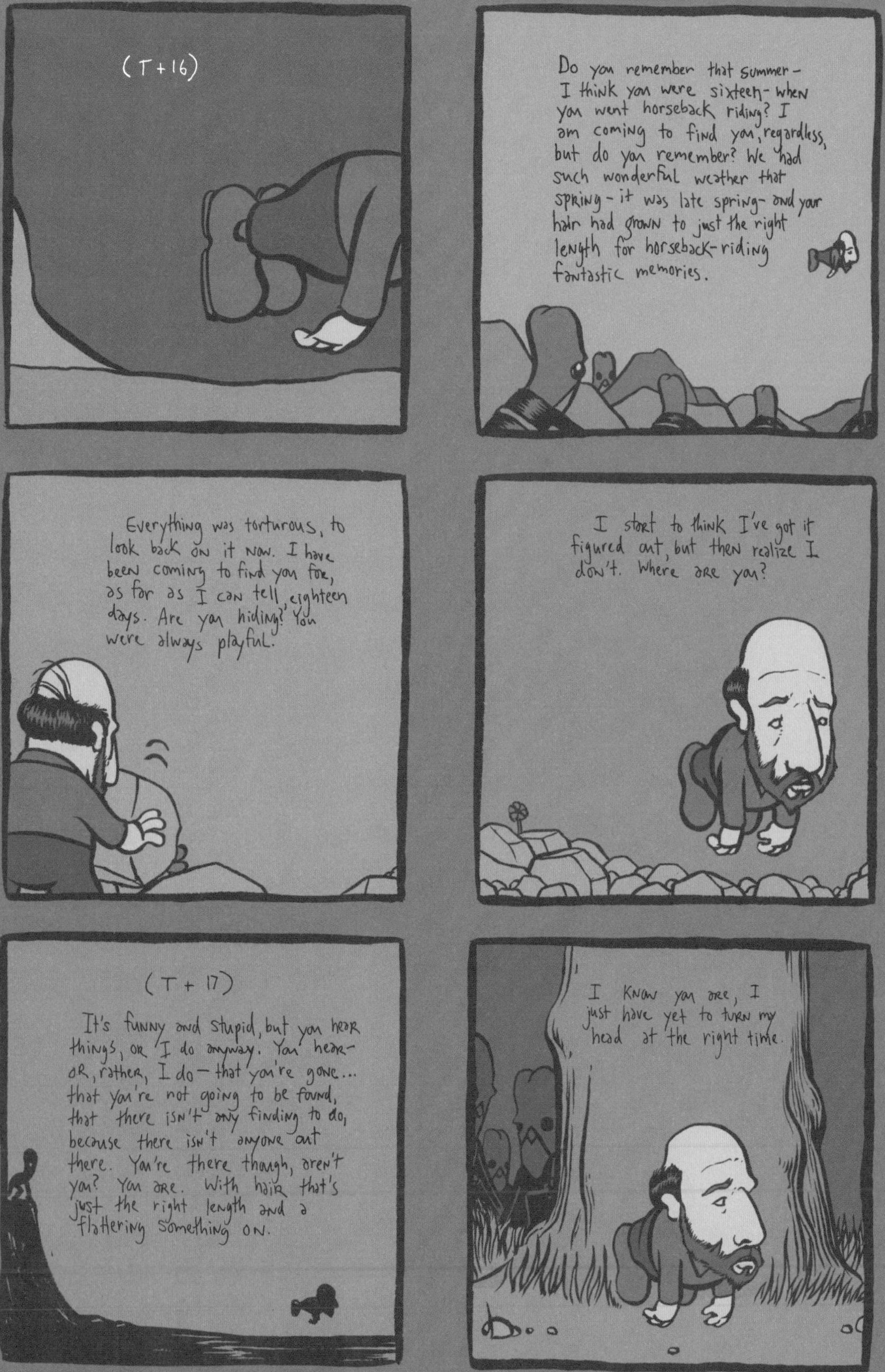
(T+16)
Do you remember that summer - I think you were sixteen - when you went horseback riding? I am coming to find you, regardless, but do you remember? We had such wonderful weather that spring - it was late spring - and your hair had grown to just the right length for horseback-riding fantastic memories.
Everything was torturous, to look back on it now. I have been coming to find you for, as far as I can tell, eighteen days. Are you hiding? You were always playful.
I start to think I've got it figured out, but then realize I don't. Where are you?
(T + 17)
It's funny and stupid, but you hear things, or I do anyway. You hear - or, rather, I do - that you're gone... that you're not going to be found, that there isn't any finding to do, because there isn't anyone out there. You're there though, aren't you? You are. With hair that's just the right length and a flattering something on.
I know you are, I just have yet to turn my head at the right time.

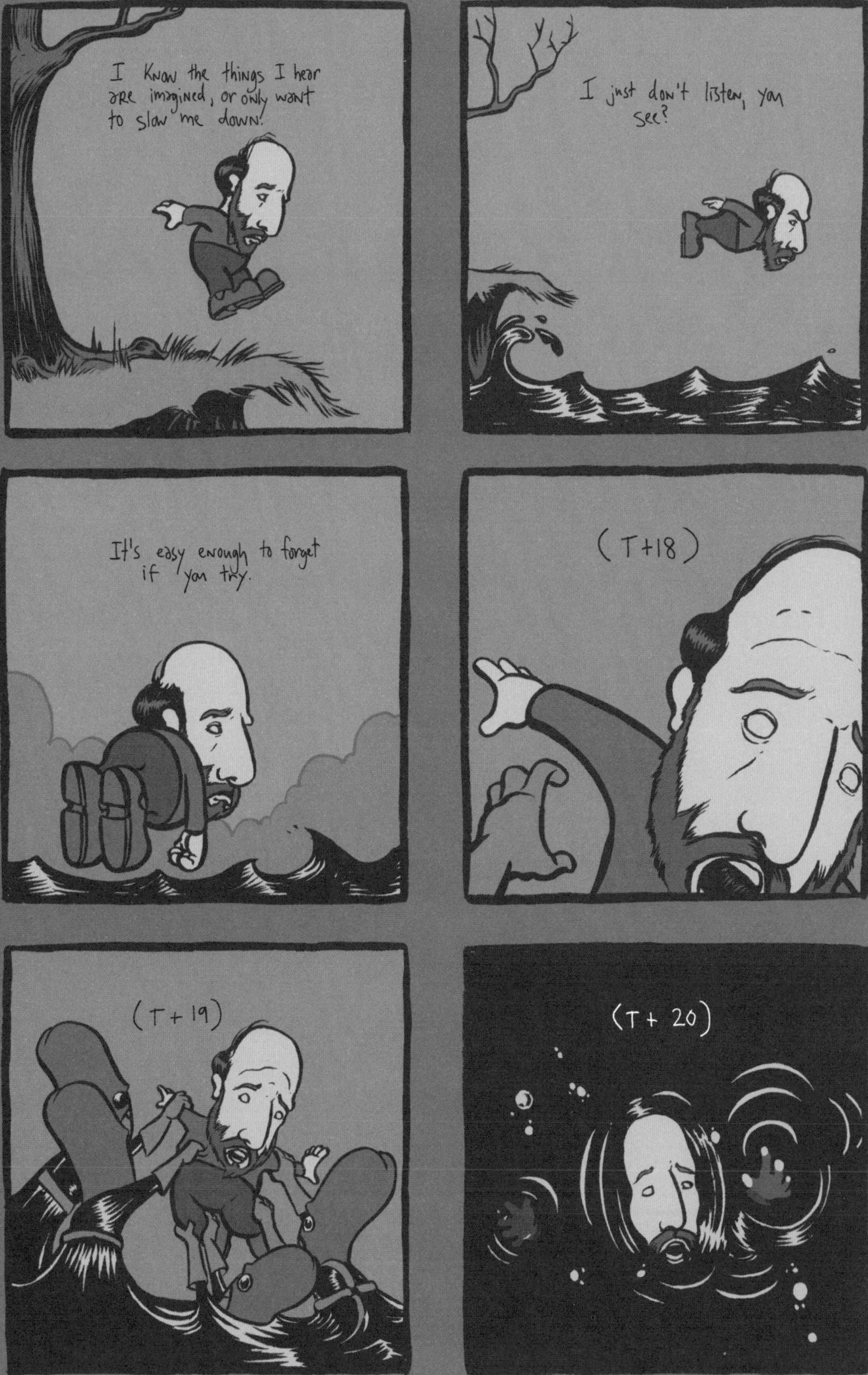
I know the things I hear are imagined, or only want to slow me down.
I just don't listen, you see?
It's easy enough to forget if you try.
(T+18)
(T+19)
(T+20)

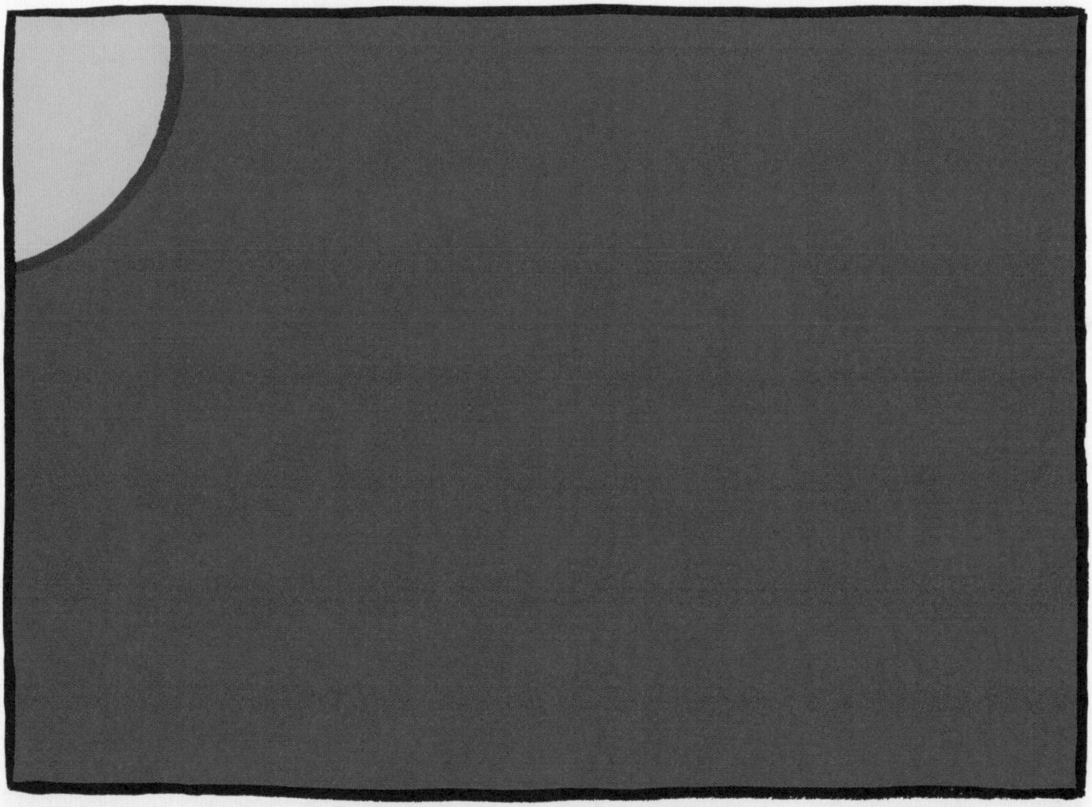

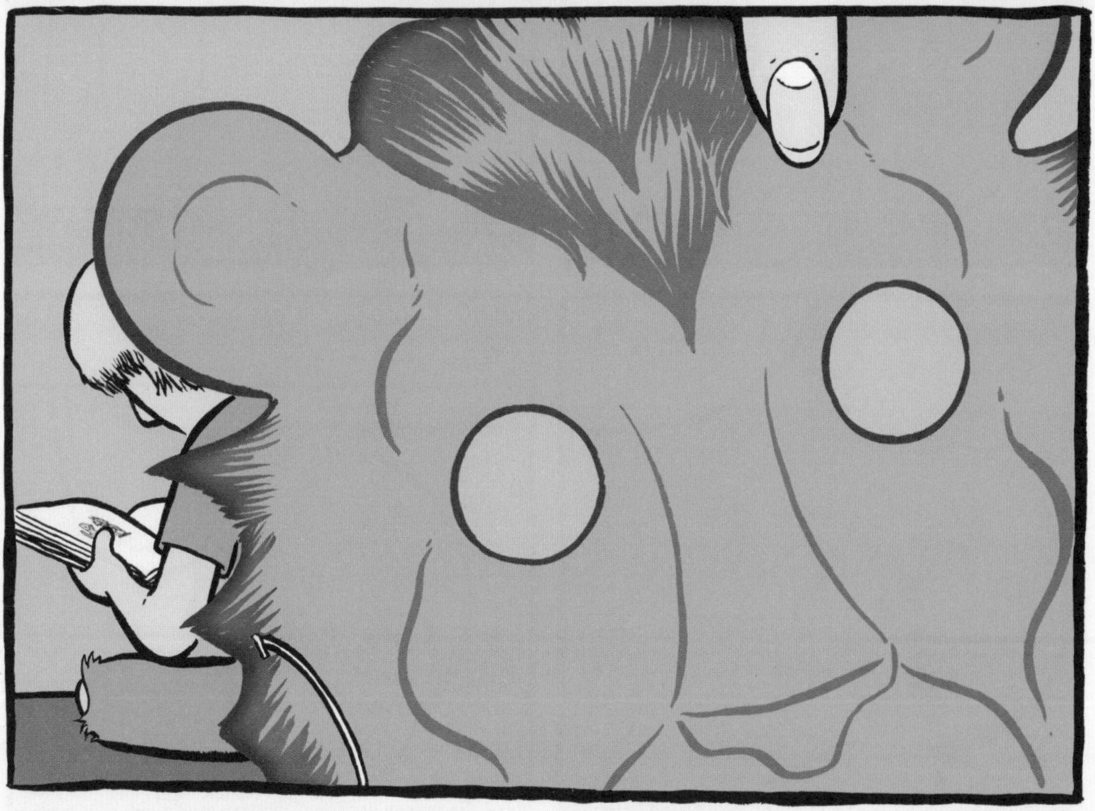

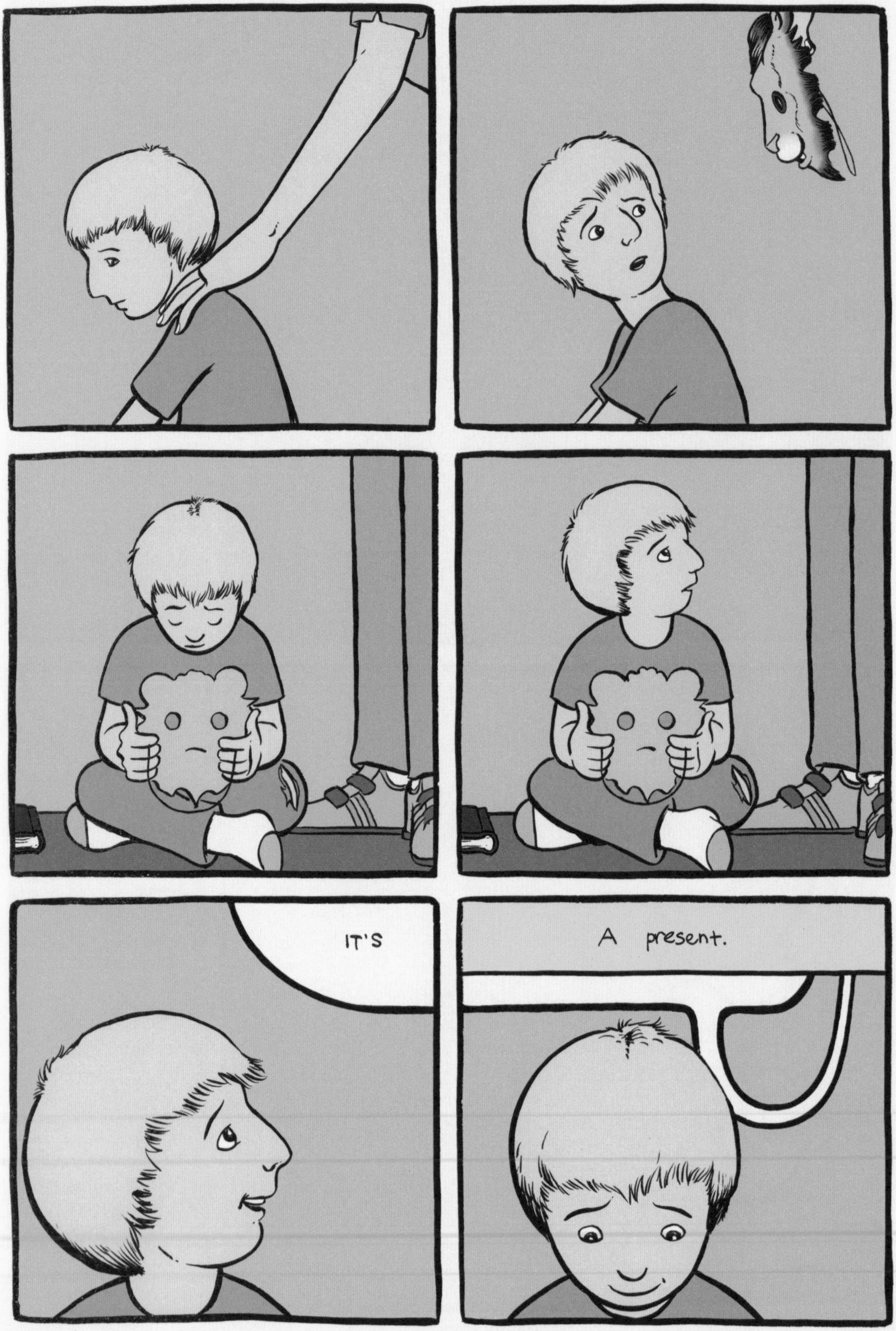

IT'S
A present.

That is ONE thing
I remember about my mother.
THANKS, MOM.

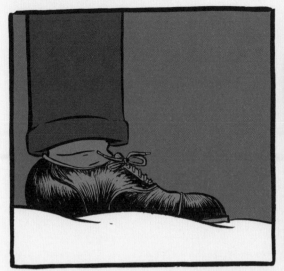

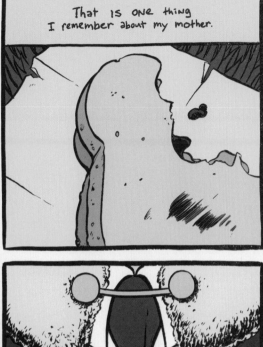

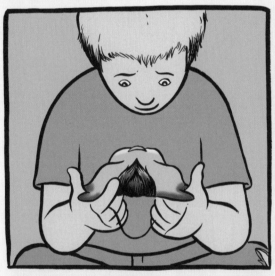

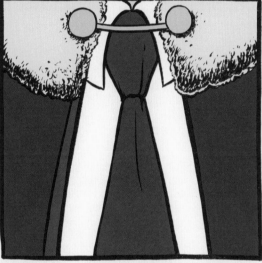

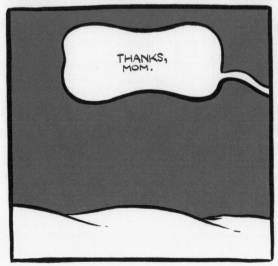

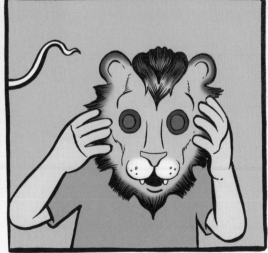

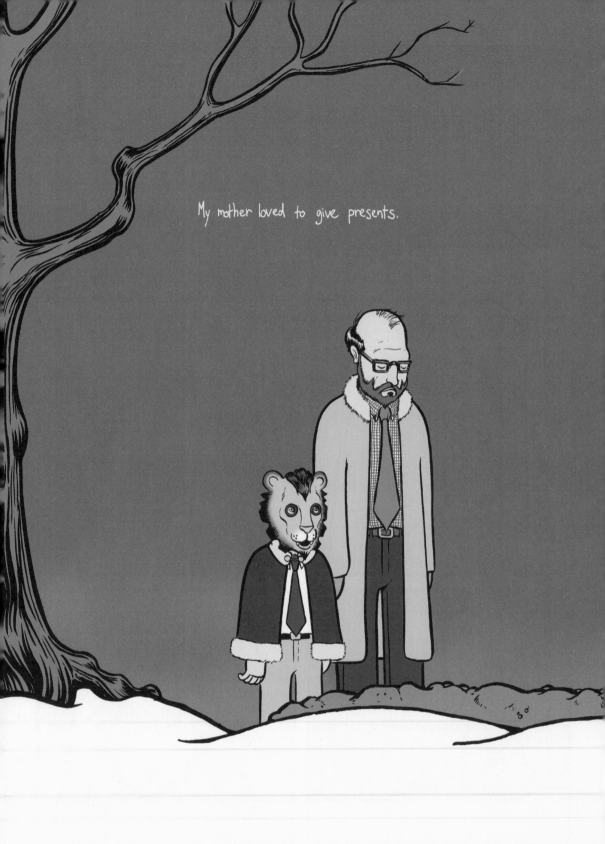

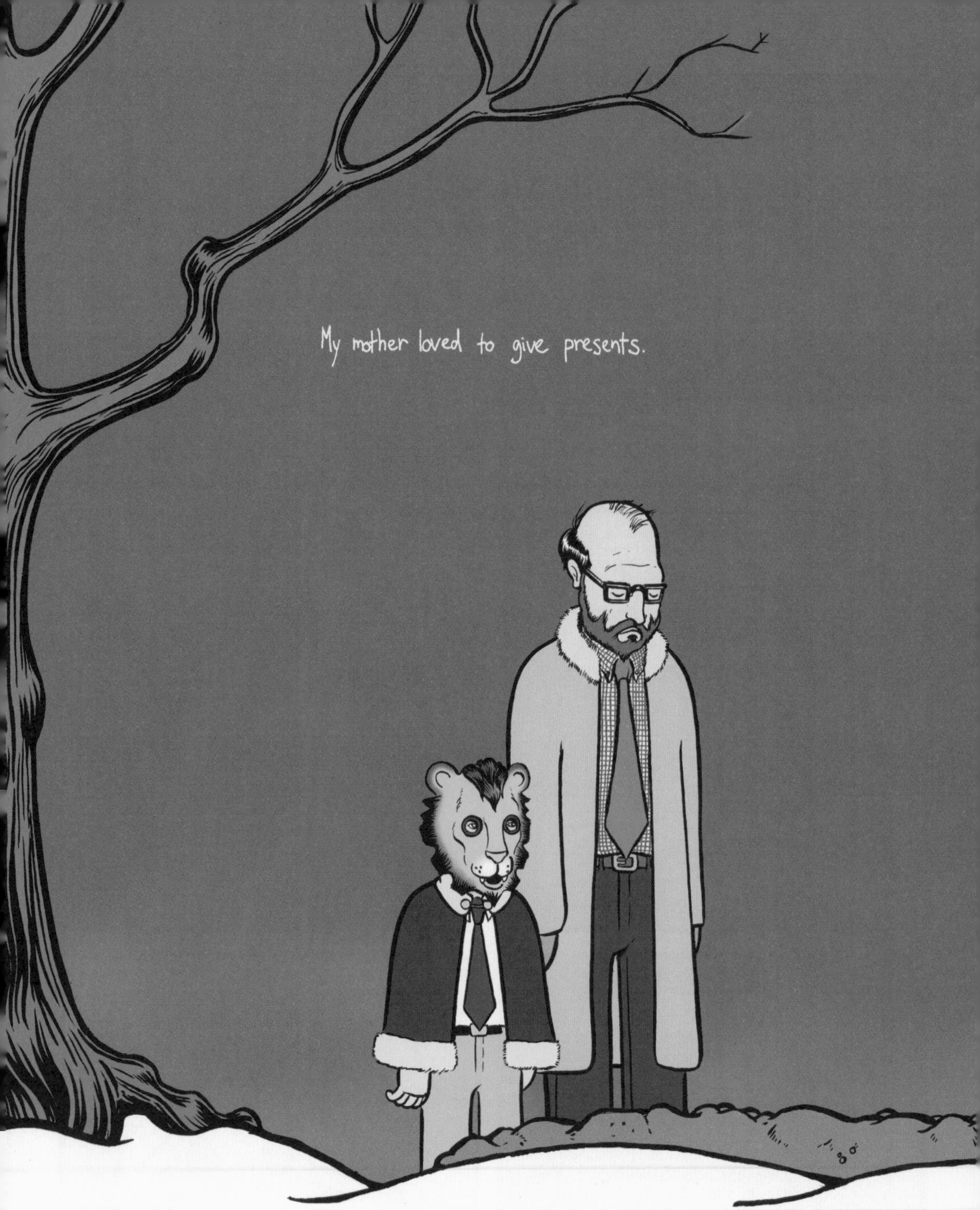
My mother loved to give presents.

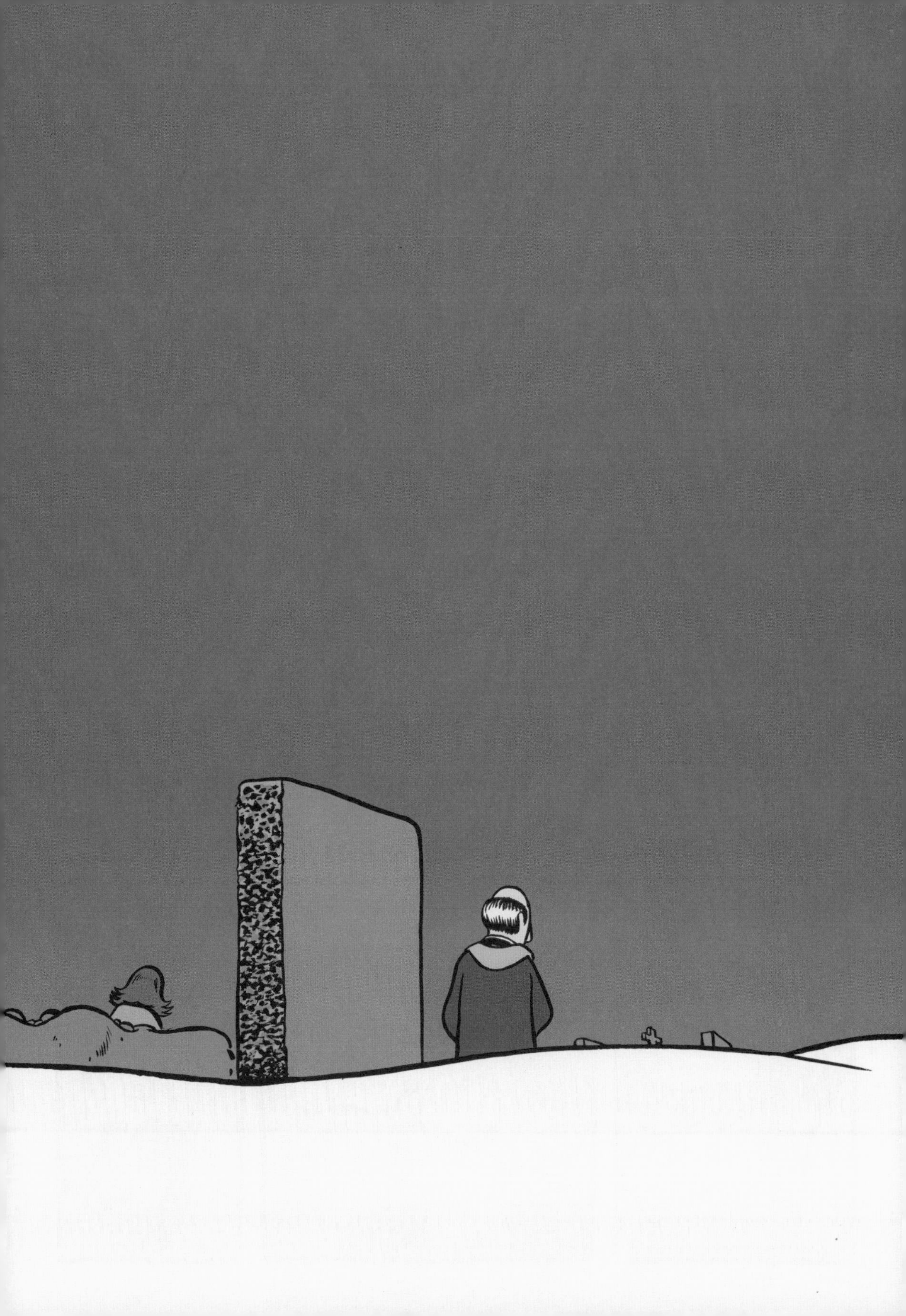

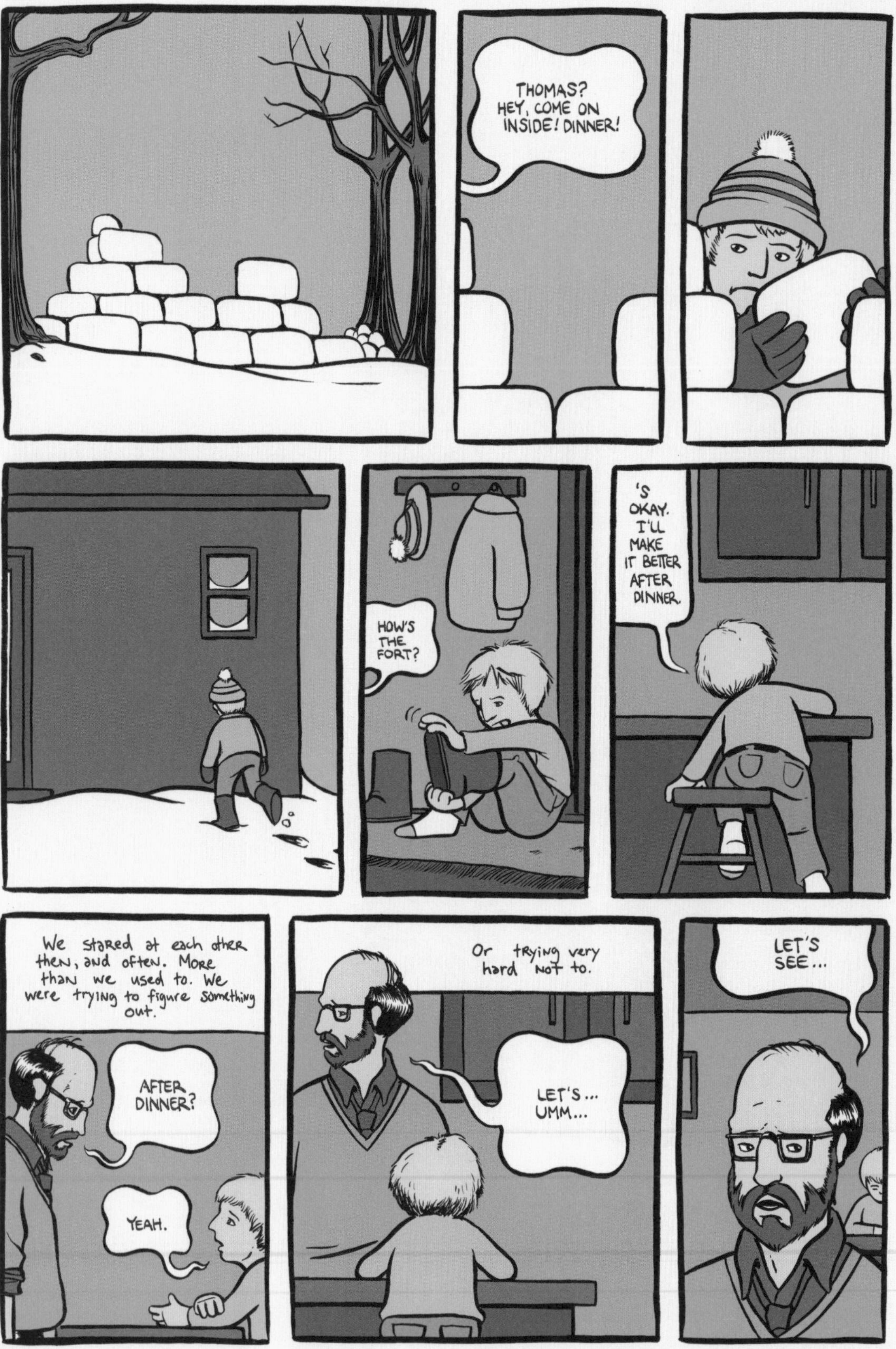
THOMAS? HEY, COME ON INSIDE! DINNER!
HOW'S THE FORT?
'S OKAY. I'LL MAKE IT BETTER AFTER DINNER.
We stared at each other then, and often. More than we used to. We were trying to figure something out.
AFTER DINNER?
YEAH.
Or trying very hard not to.
LET'S... UMM...
LET'S SEE...

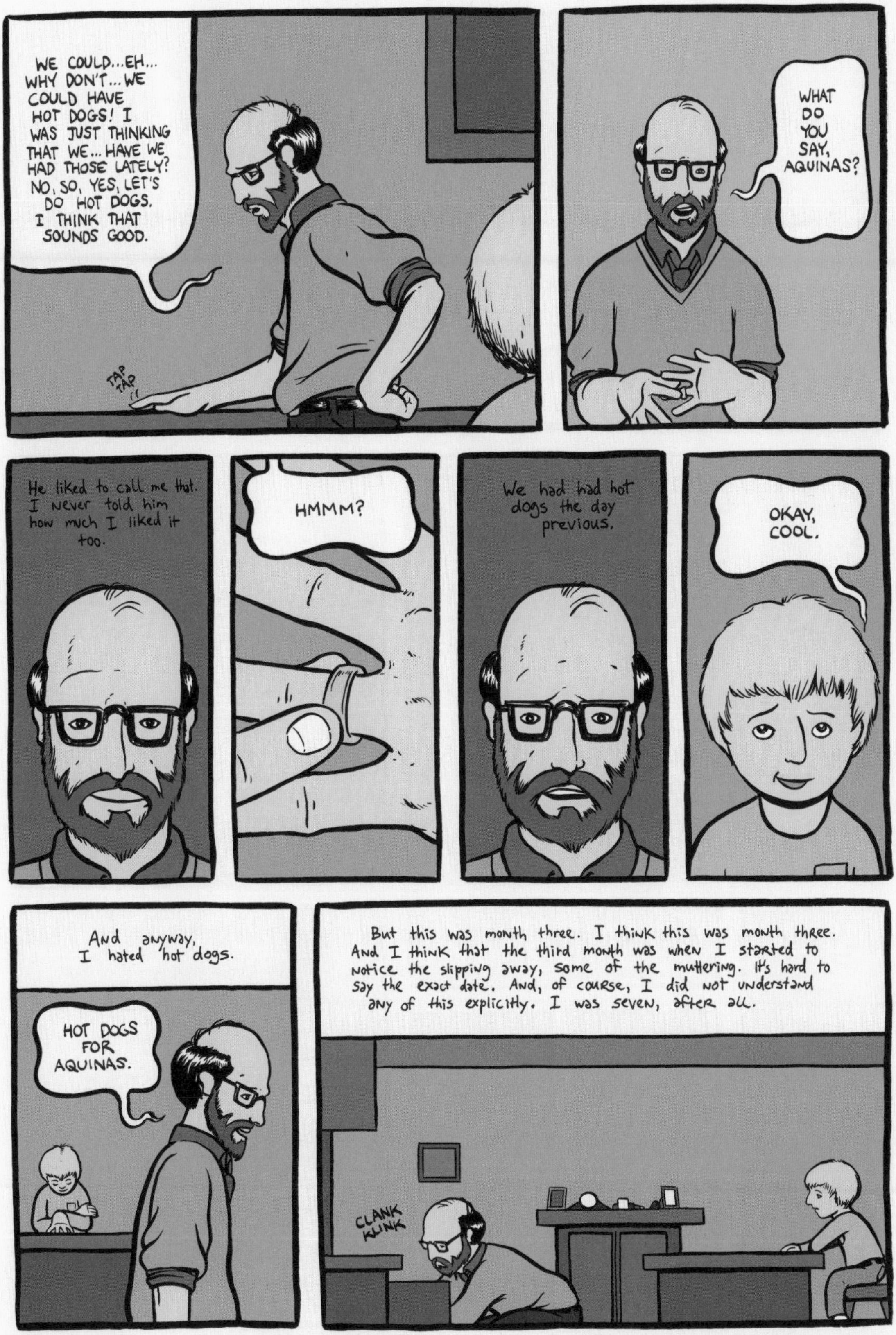

WE COULD...EH... WHY DON'T...WE COULD HAVE HOT DOGS! I WAS JUST THINKING THAT WE... HAVE WE HAD THOSE LATELY? NO, SO, YES, LET'S DO HOT DOGS. I THINK THAT SOUNDS GOOD.
TAP TAP
WHAT DO YOU SAY, AQUINAS?
He liked to call me that. I never told him how much I liked it too.
HMMM?
We had had hot dogs the day previous.
OKAY, COOL.
And anyway, I hated hot dogs.
HOT DOGS FOR AQUINAS.
But this was month three. I think this was month three. And I think that the third month was when I started to notice the slipping away, some of the muttering. It's hard to say the exact date. And, of course, I did not understand any of this explicitly. I was seven, after all.
CLANK KLINK

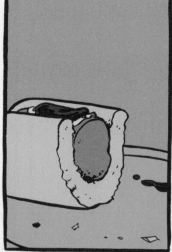

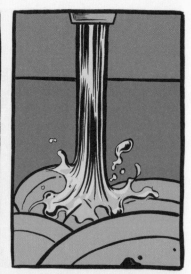

And I was busy with matters of my own.

KLINK

I was, in her absence, the groundskeeper, and these were my grounds:

Her garden, her room, her hiding place, the woods between.

These were the areas over which I kept watch. These were significant areas, though the importance is muddled through a seven year-old's screen. Still, the sentiment common to all was all too clear: these were too powerfully **HERS**, and my father would not go near them.

So I kept them.

THE GARDEN

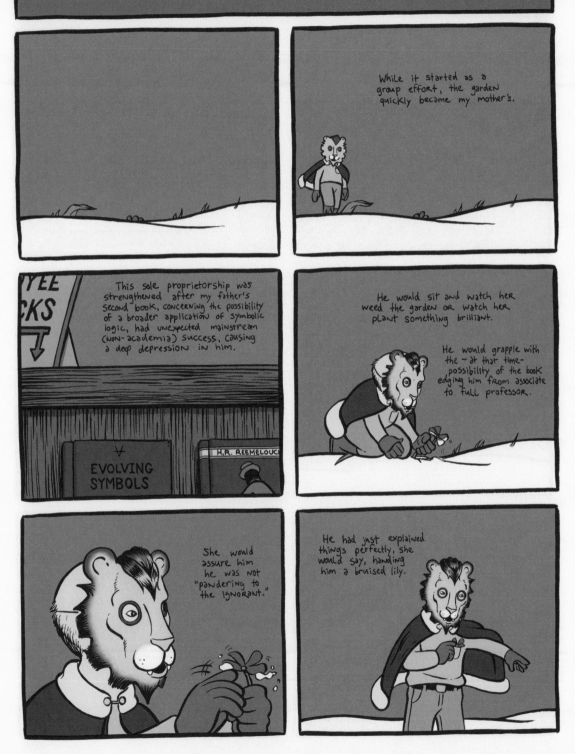

While it started as a group effort, the garden quickly became my mother's.

This sole proprietorship was strengthened after my father's second book, concerning the possibility of a broader application of symbolic logic, had unexpected mainstream (non-academia) success, causing a deep depression in him.

EVOLVING SYMBOLS

H.R. REEMELOUC

He would sit and watch her weed the garden or watch her plant something brilliant.

He would grapple with the ~ at that time-possibility of the book edging him from associate to full professor.

She would assure him he was not "pandering to the ignorant."

He had just explained things perfectly, she would say, handing him a bruised lily.

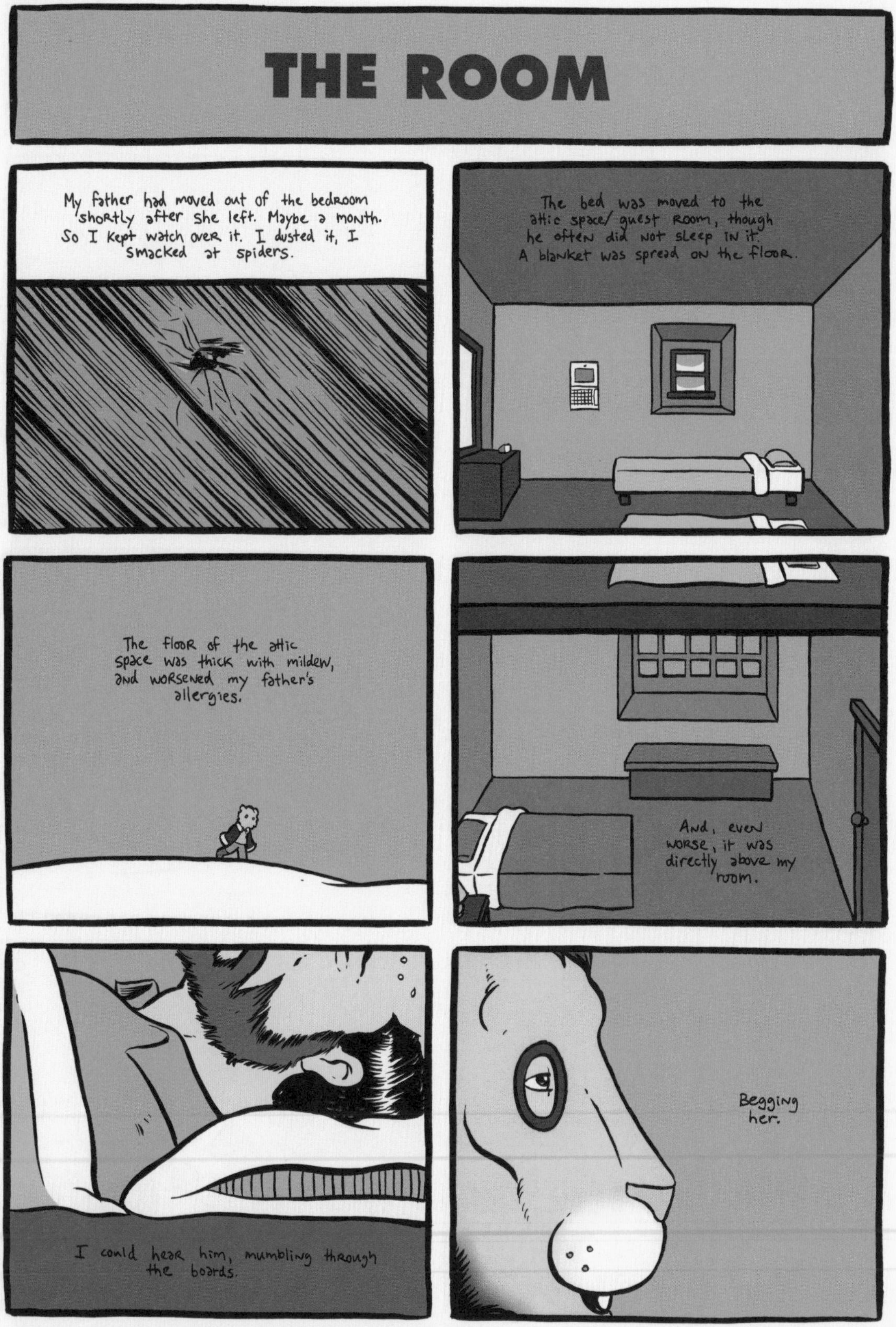
THE ROOM
My father had moved out of the bedroom shortly after she left. Maybe a month. So I kept watch over it. I dusted it, I smacked at spiders.
The bed was moved to the attic space/ guest room, though he often did not sleep in it. A blanket was spread on the floor.
The floor of the attic space was thick with mildew, and worsened my father's allergies.
And, even worse, it was directly above my room.
I could hear him, mumbling through the boards.
Begging her.

THE HIDING PLACE

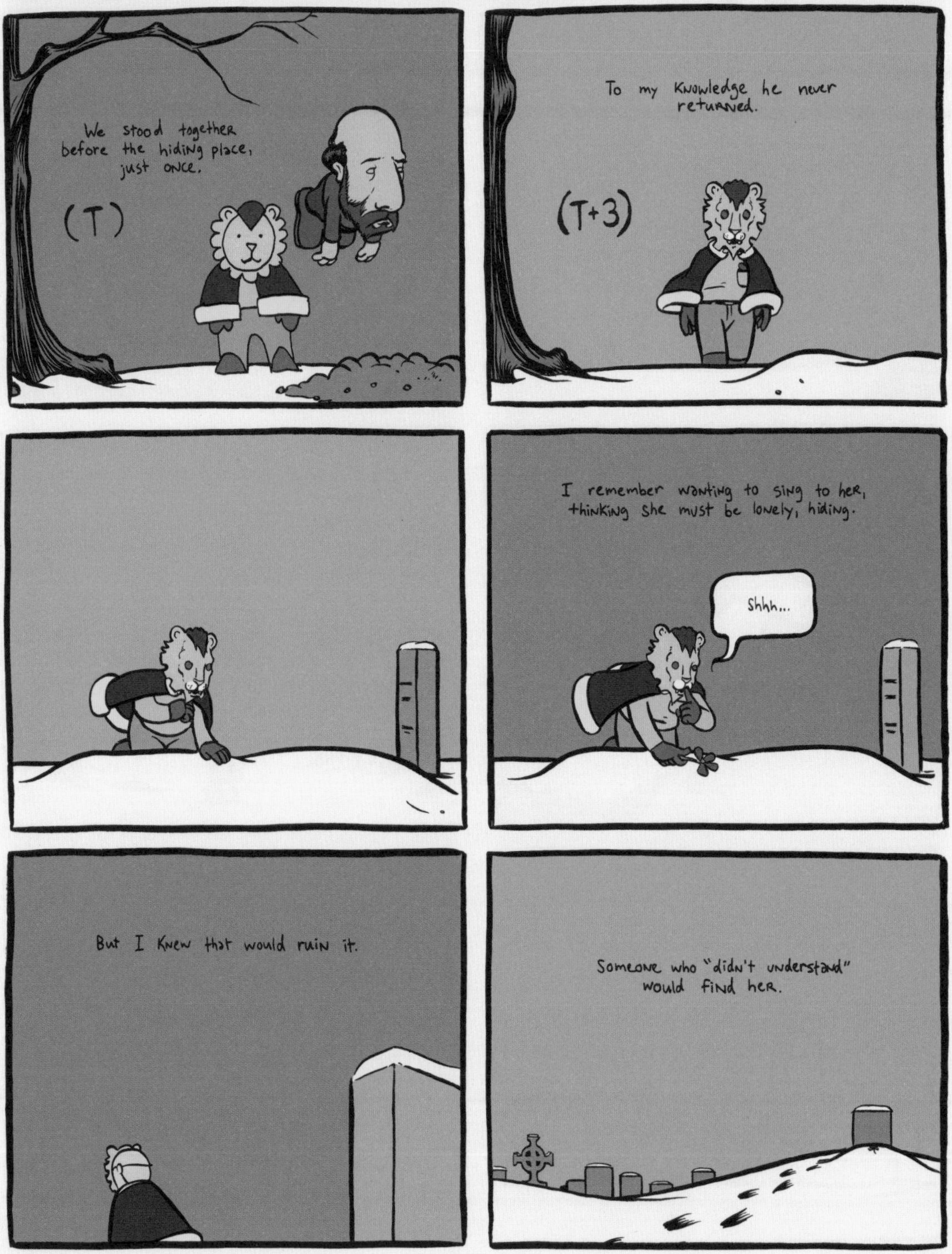
We stood together before the hiding place, just once.
(T)
To my knowledge he never returned.
(T+3)
I remember wanting to sing to her, thinking she must be lonely, hiding.
Shhh...
But I knew that would ruin it.
Someone who "didn't understand" would find her.

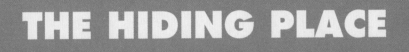

THE WOODS BETWEEN

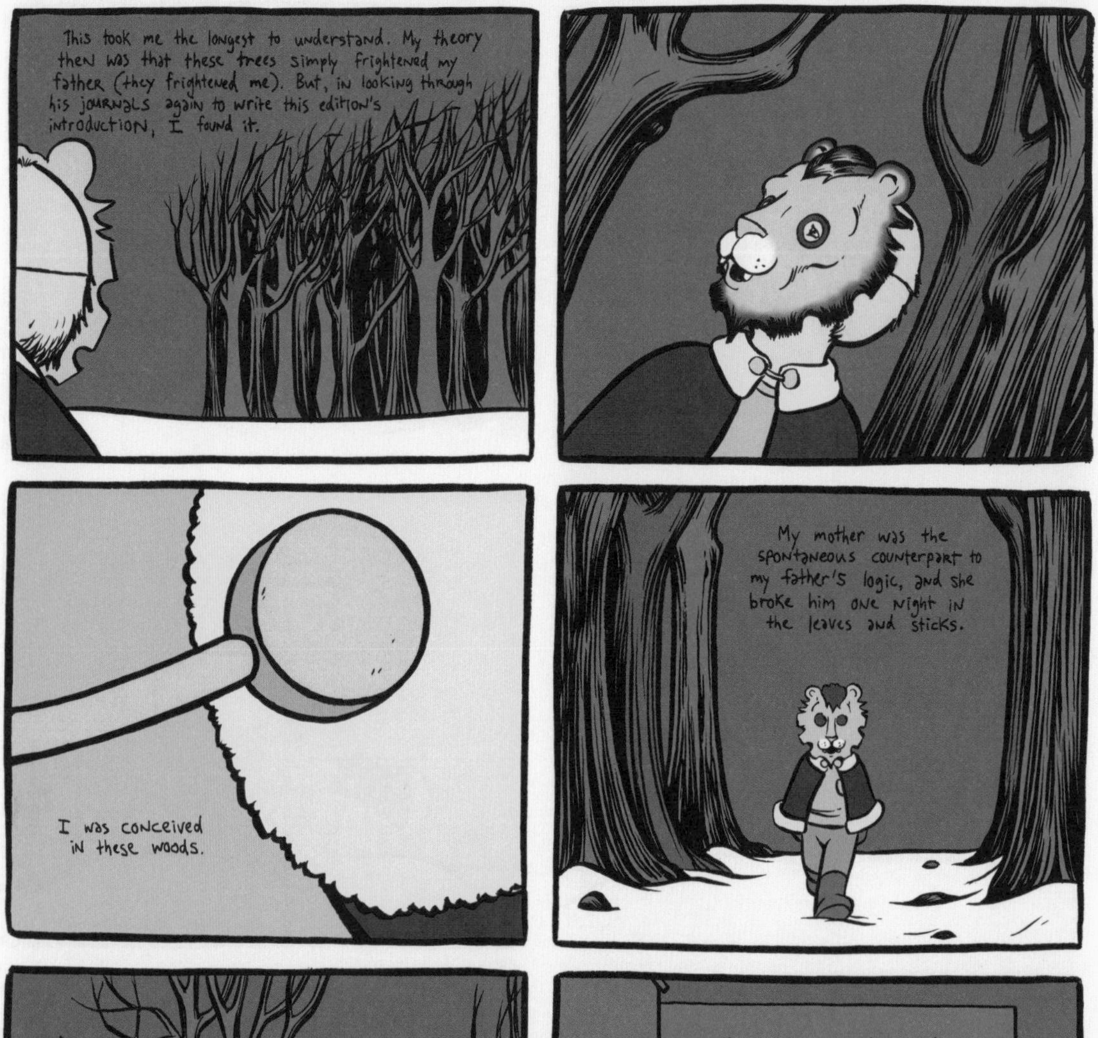

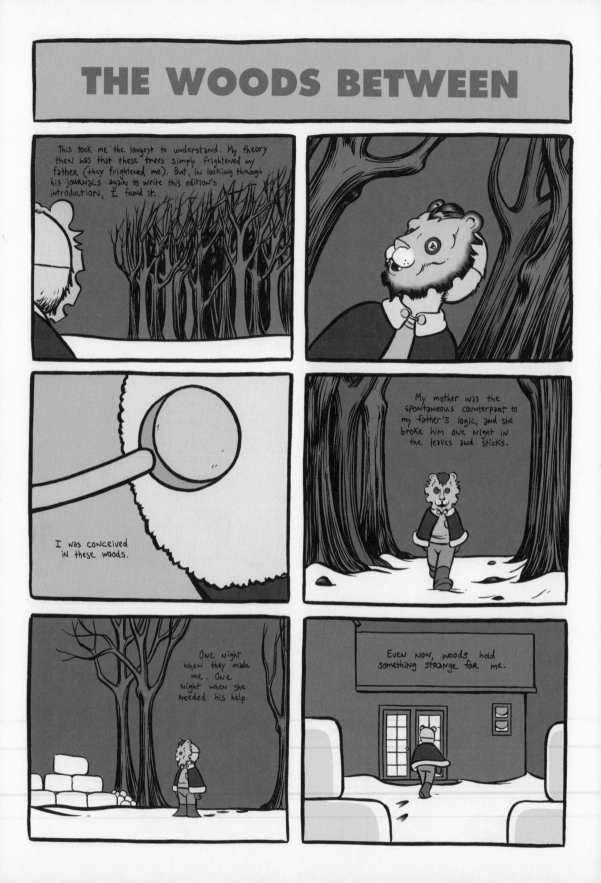

This took me the longest to understand. My theory then was that these trees simply frightened my father (they frightened me). But, in looking through his journals again to write this edition's introduction, I found it.
I was conceived in these woods.
My mother was the spontaneous counterpart to my father's logic, and she broke him one night in the leaves and sticks.
One night when they made me. One night when she needed his help.
Even now, woods hold something strange for me.

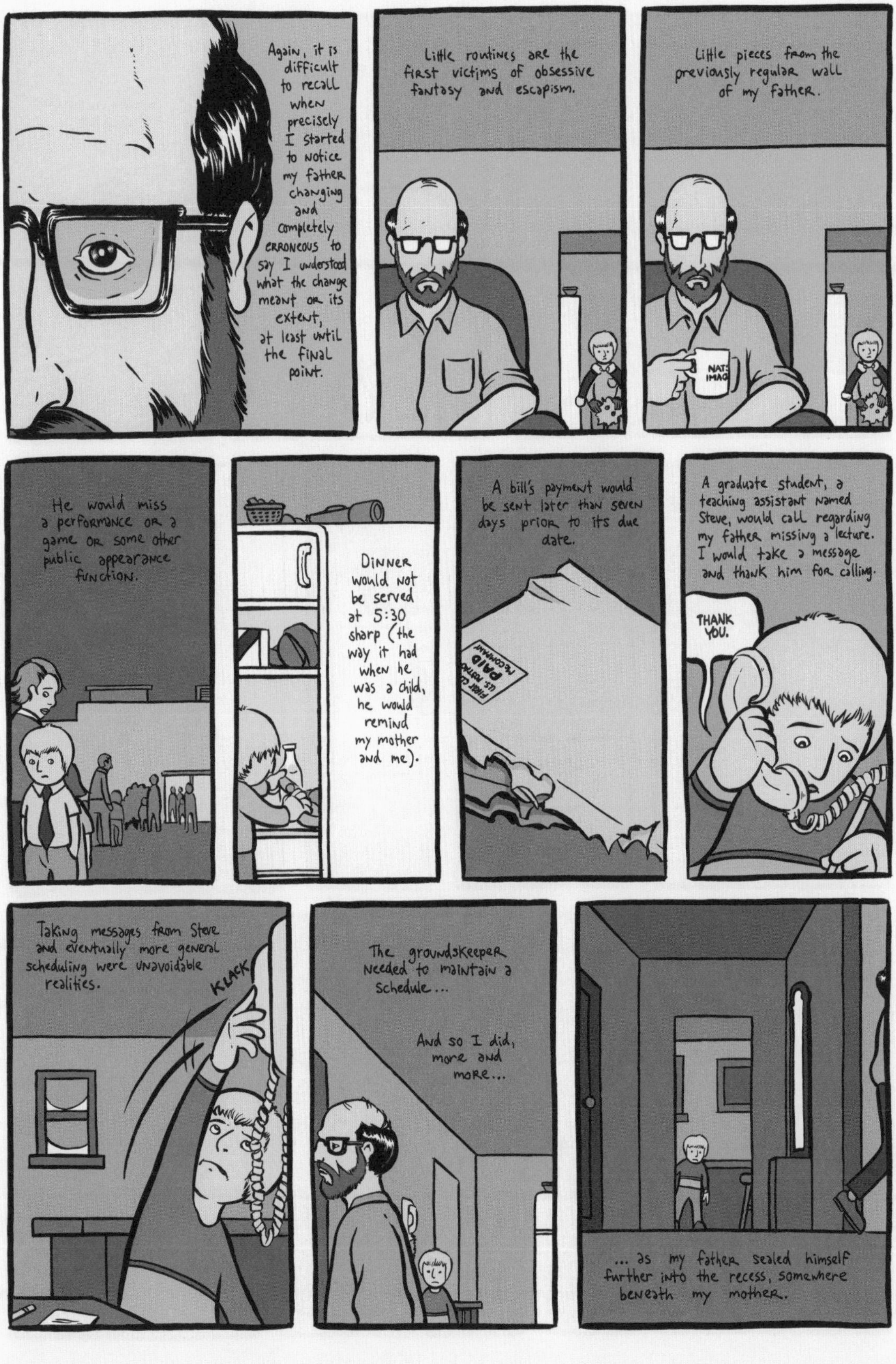
Again, it is difficult to recall when precisely I started to notice my father changing and completely erroneous to say I understood what the change meant or its extent, at least until the final point.
Little routines are the first victims of obsessive fantasy and escapism.
Little pieces from the previously regular wall of my father.
He would miss a performance or a game or some other public appearance function.
Dinner would not be served at 5:30 sharp (the way it had when he was a child, he would remind my mother and me).
A bill's payment would be sent later than seven days prior to its due date.
PAID
A graduate student, a teaching assistant named Steve, would call regarding my father missing a lecture. I would take a message and thank him for calling.
THANK YOU.
Taking messages from Steve and eventually more general scheduling were unavoidable realities.
KLACK
The groundskeeper needed to maintain a schedule...
And so I did, more and more...
... as my father sealed himself further into the recess, somewhere beneath my mother.

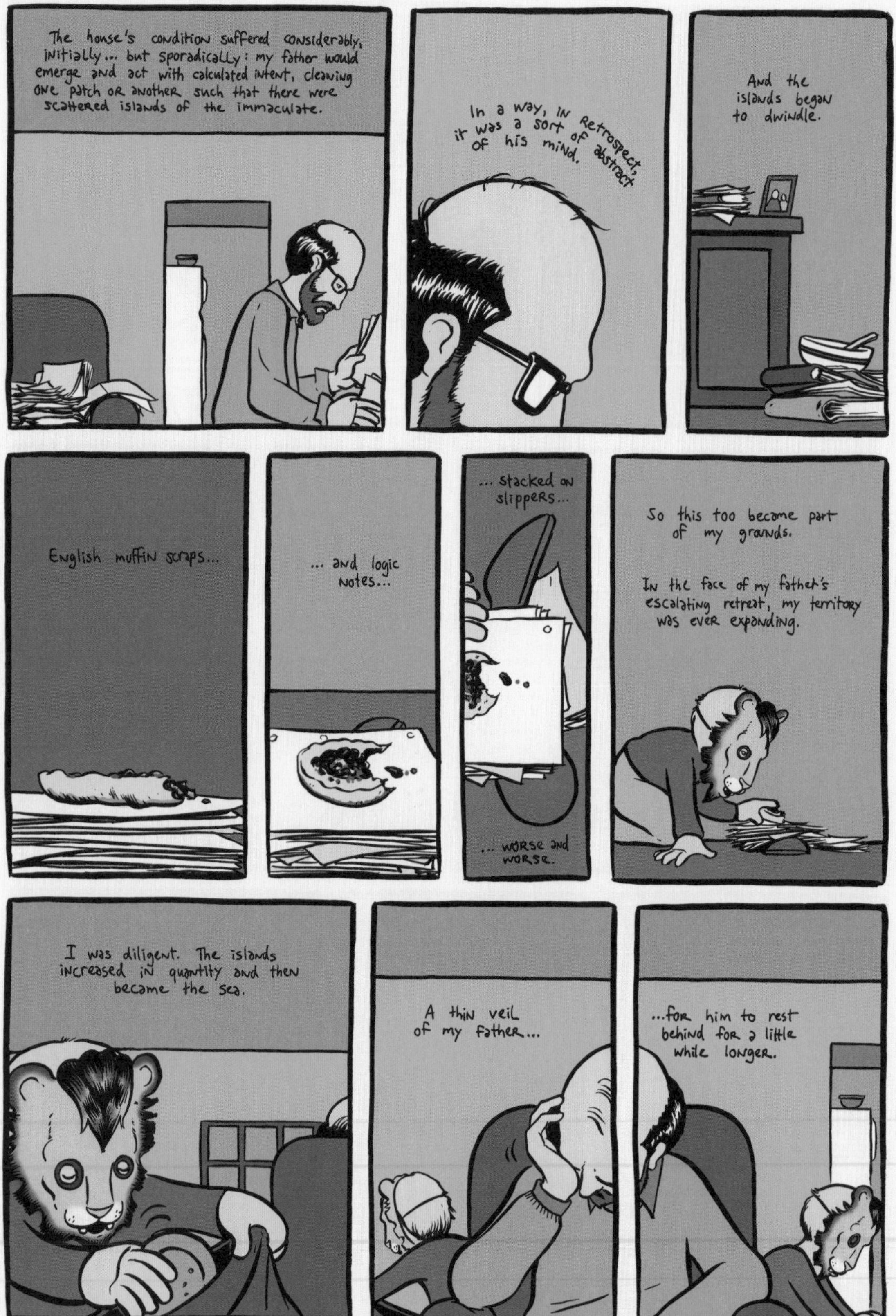

The house's condition suffered considerably, initially... but sporadically: my father would emerge and act with calculated intent, cleaning one patch or another such that there were scattered islands of the immaculate.
In a way, in retrospect, it was a sort of abstract of his mind.
And the islands began to dwindle.
English muffin scraps...
... and logic notes...
... stacked on slippers...
... worse and worse.
So this too became part of my grounds.
In the face of my father's escalating retreat, my territory was ever expanding.
I was diligent. The islands increased in quantity and then became the sea.
A thin veil of my father...
...for him to rest behind for a little while longer.

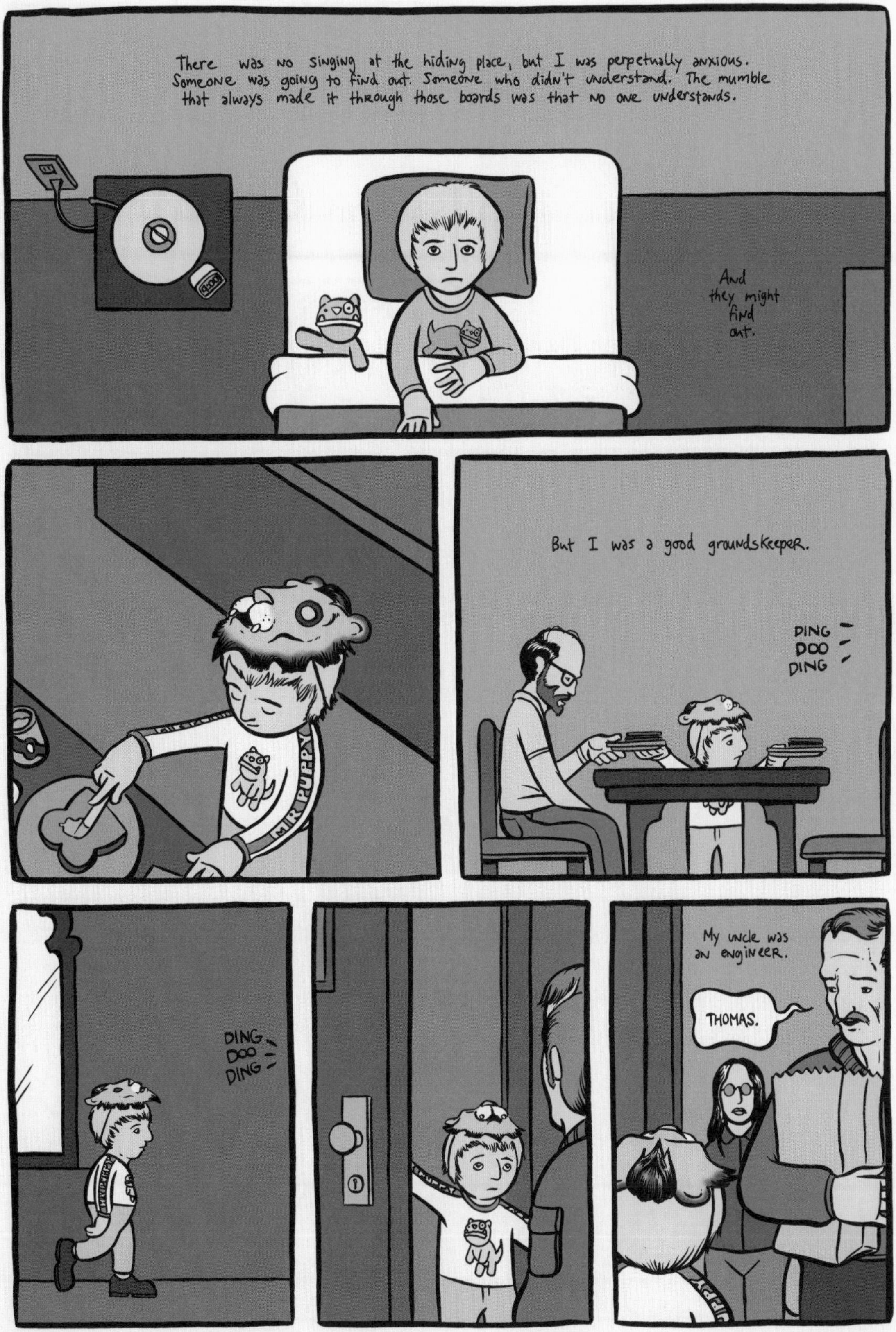
There was no singing at the hiding place, but I was perpetually anxious. Someone was going to find out. Someone who didn't understand. The mumble that always made it through those boards was that no one understands.
And they might find out.
MR PUPPY
But I was a good groundskeeper.
DING DOO DING
DING DOO DING
My uncle was an engineer.
THOMAS.

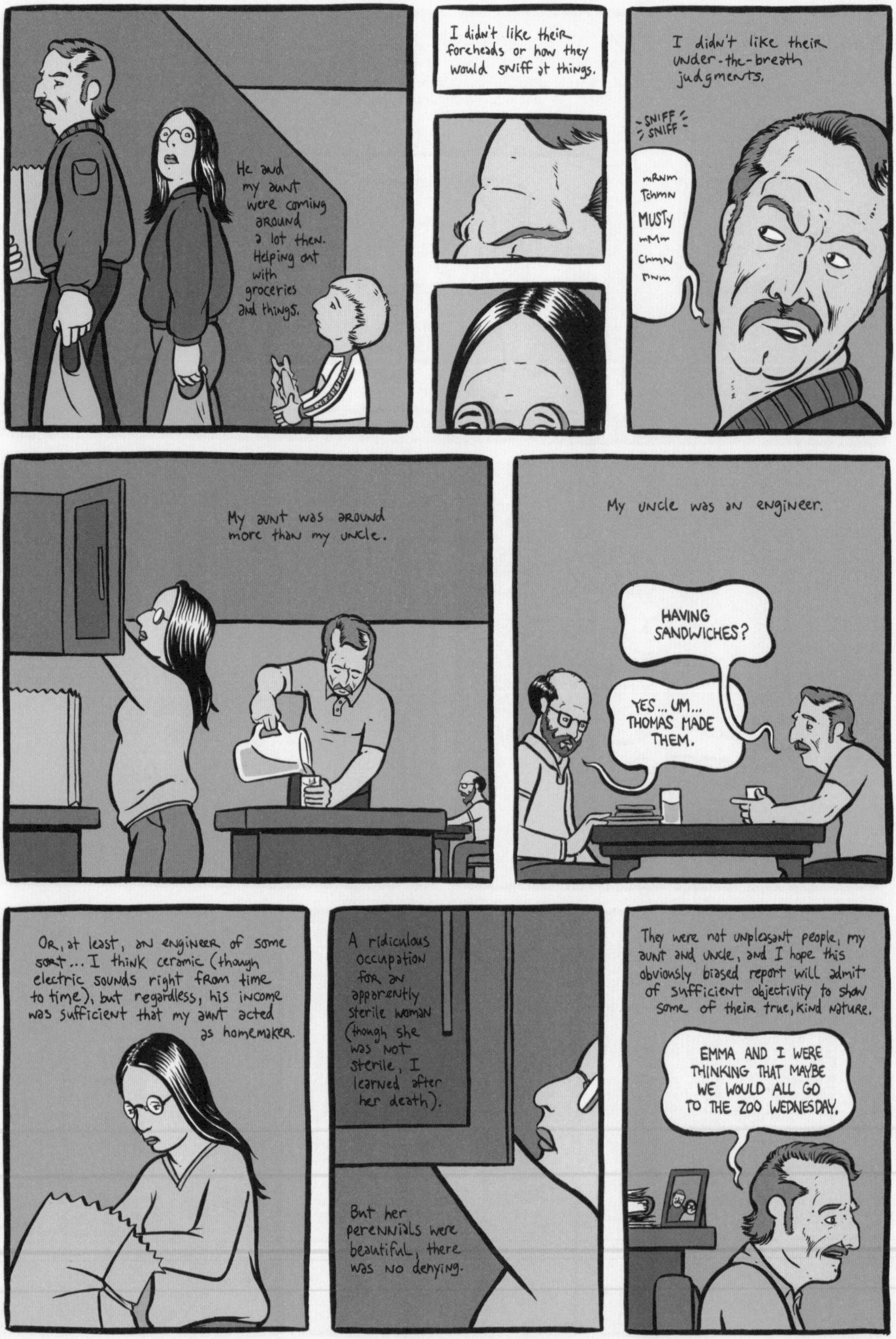
He and my aunt were coming around a lot then. Helping out with groceries and things.
I didn't like their foreheads or how they would sniff at things.
I didn't like their under-the-breath judgments.
SNIFF SNIFF
MUSTy
My aunt was around more than my uncle.
My uncle was an engineer.
HAVING SANDWICHES?
YES... UM... THOMAS MADE THEM.
Or, at least, an engineer of some sort... I think ceramic (though electric sounds right from time to time), but regardless, his income was sufficient that my aunt acted as homemaker.
A ridiculous occupation for an apparently sterile woman (though she was not sterile, I learned after her death).
But her perennials were beautiful, there was no denying.
They were not unpleasant people, my aunt and uncle, and I hope this obviously biased report will admit of sufficient objectivity to show some of their true, kind nature.
EMMA AND I WERE THINKING THAT MAYBE WE WOULD ALL GO TO THE ZOO WEDNESDAY.

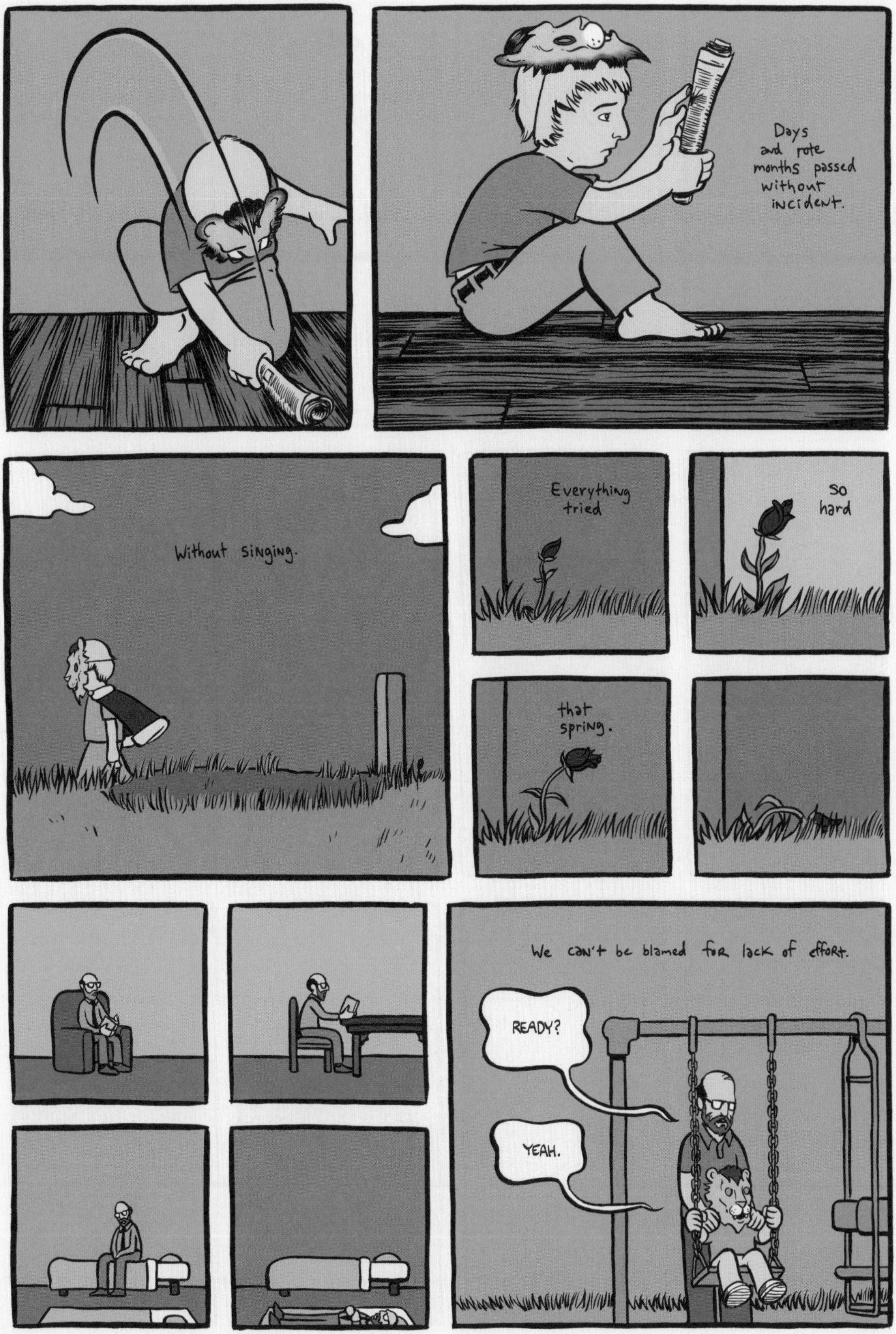
Days and rote months passed without incident.
Without singing.
Everything tried
so hard
that spring.
We can't be blamed for lack of effort.
READY?
YEAH.

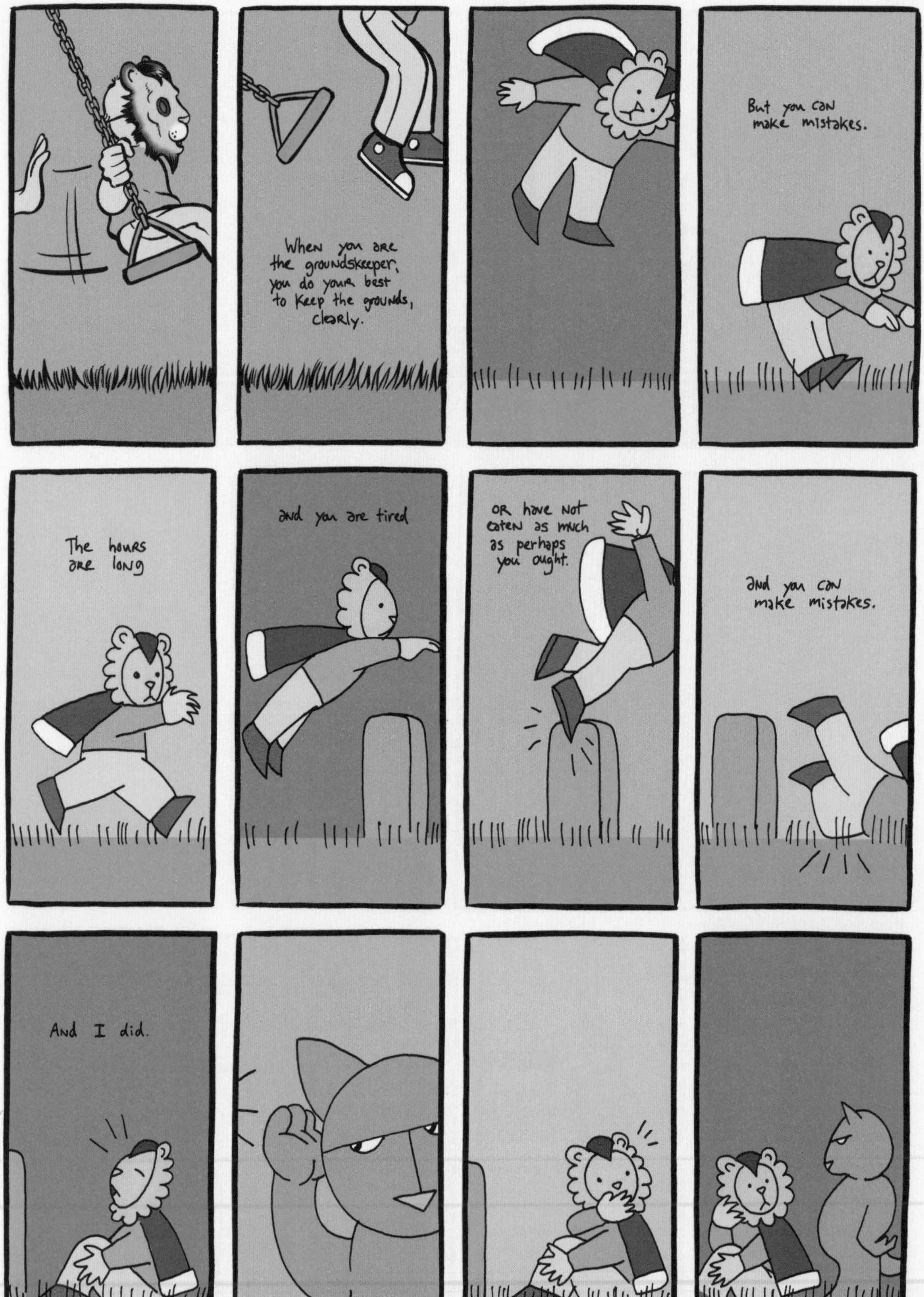

When you are the groundskeeper, you do your best to keep the grounds, clearly.
But you can make mistakes.
The hours are long
and you are tired
or have not eaten as much as perhaps you ought.
and you can make mistakes.
And I did.

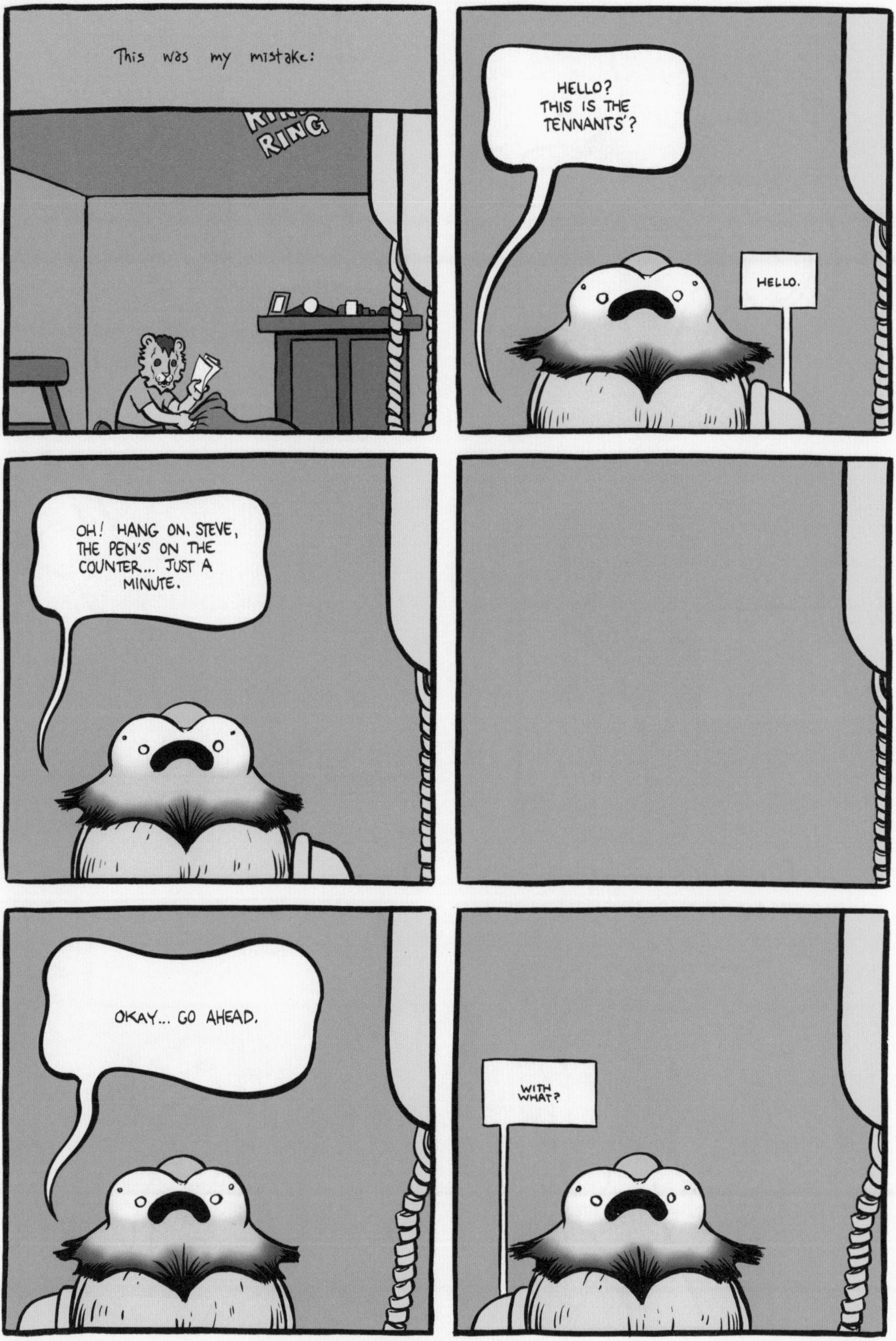
This was my mistake:
RING RING
HELLO? THIS IS THE TENNANTS'?
HELLO.
OH! HANG ON, STEVE, THE PEN'S ON THE COUNTER... JUST A MINUTE.
OKAY... GO AHEAD.
WITH WHAT?

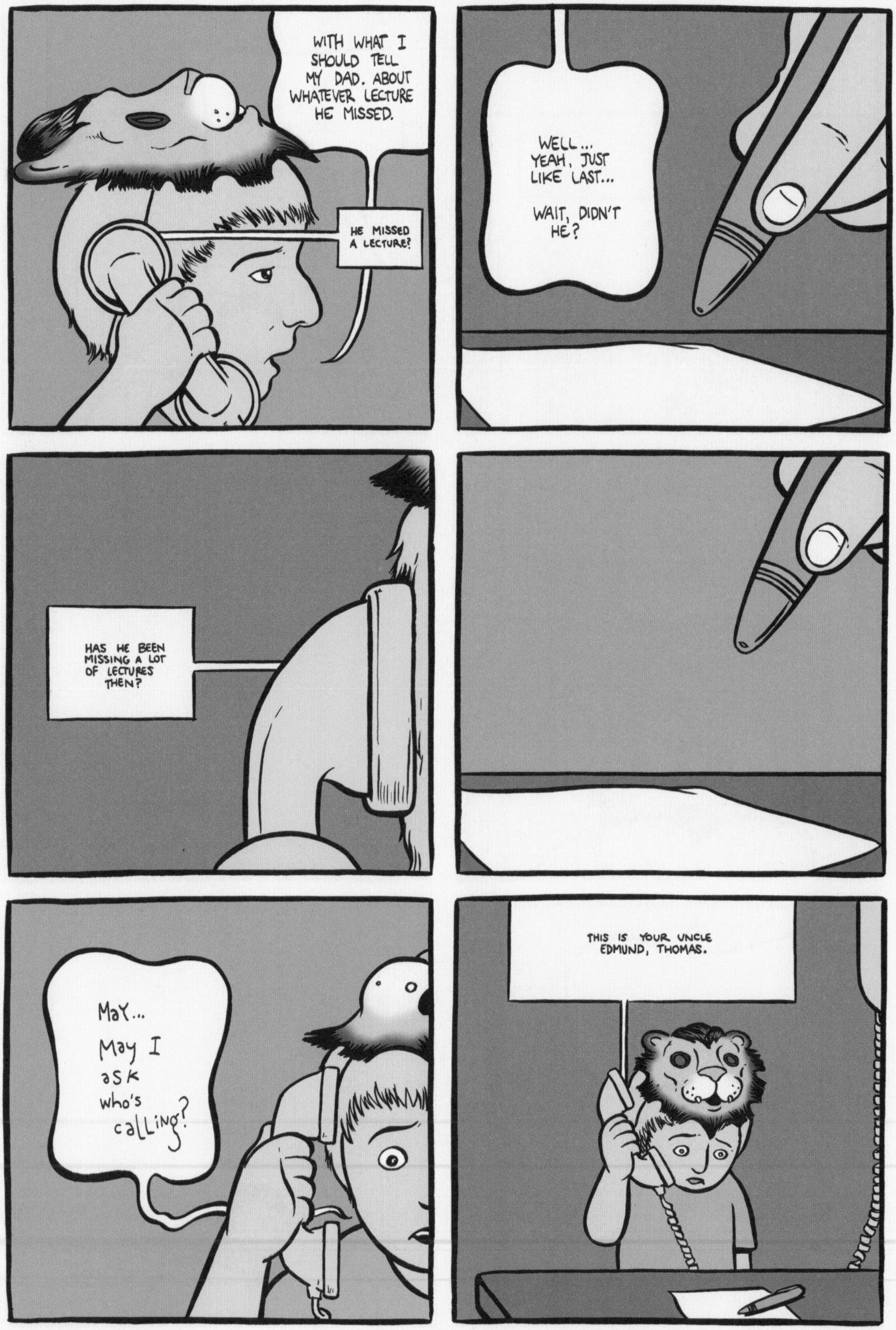
WITH WHAT I SHOULD TELL MY DAD. ABOUT WHATEVER LECTURE HE MISSED.
HE MISSED A LECTURE?
WELL... YEAH, JUST LIKE LAST...
WAIT, DIDN'T HE?
HAS HE BEEN MISSING A LOT OF LECTURES THEN?
May...
May I ask who's calling?
THIS IS YOUR UNCLE EDMUND, THOMAS.

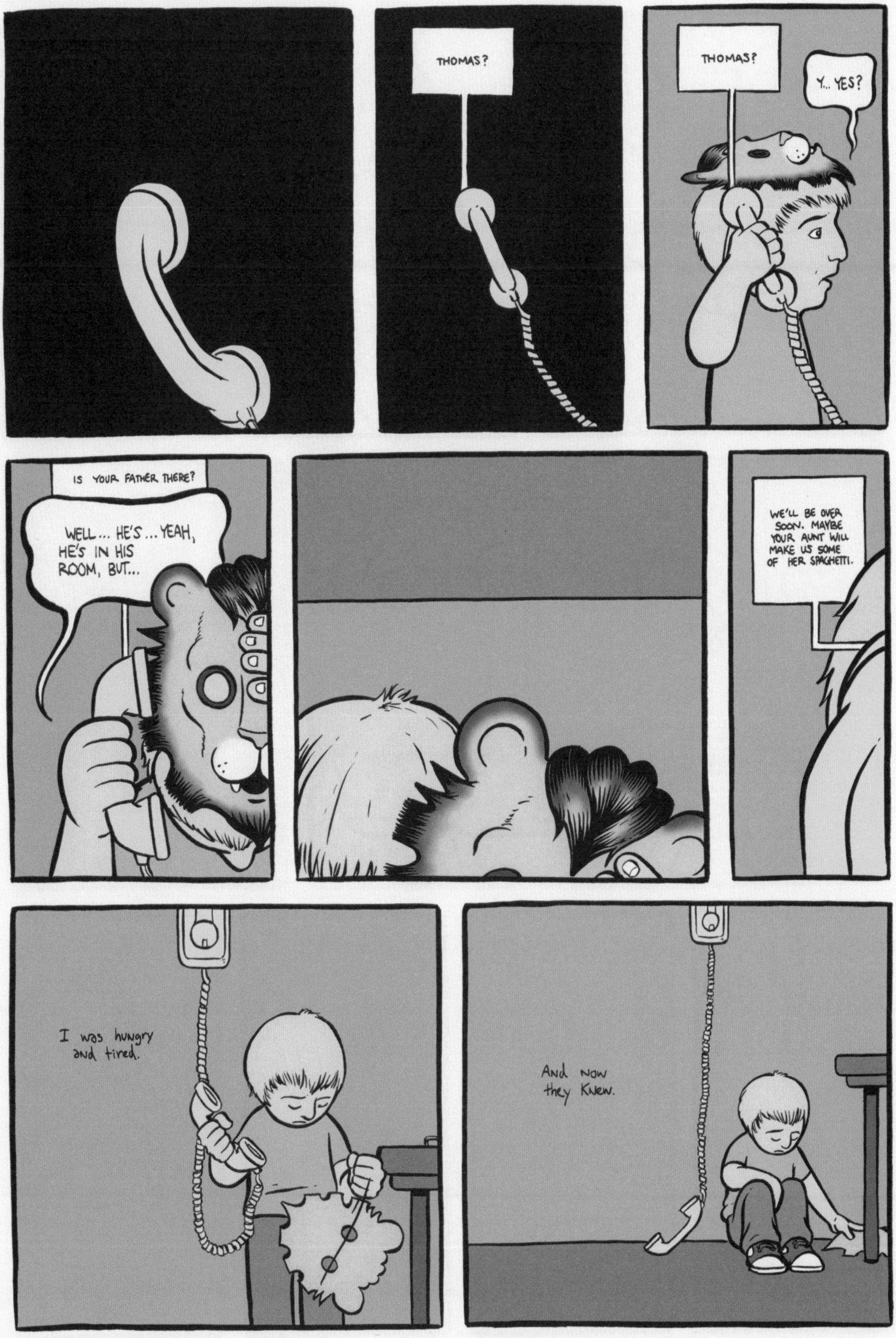
THOMAS?
THOMAS?
Y... YES?
IS YOUR FATHER THERE?
WELL... HE'S ... YEAH, HE'S IN HIS ROOM, BUT...
WE'LL BE OVER SOON. MAYBE YOUR AUNT WILL MAKE US SOME OF HER SPAGHETTI.
I was hungry and tired.
And now they knew.

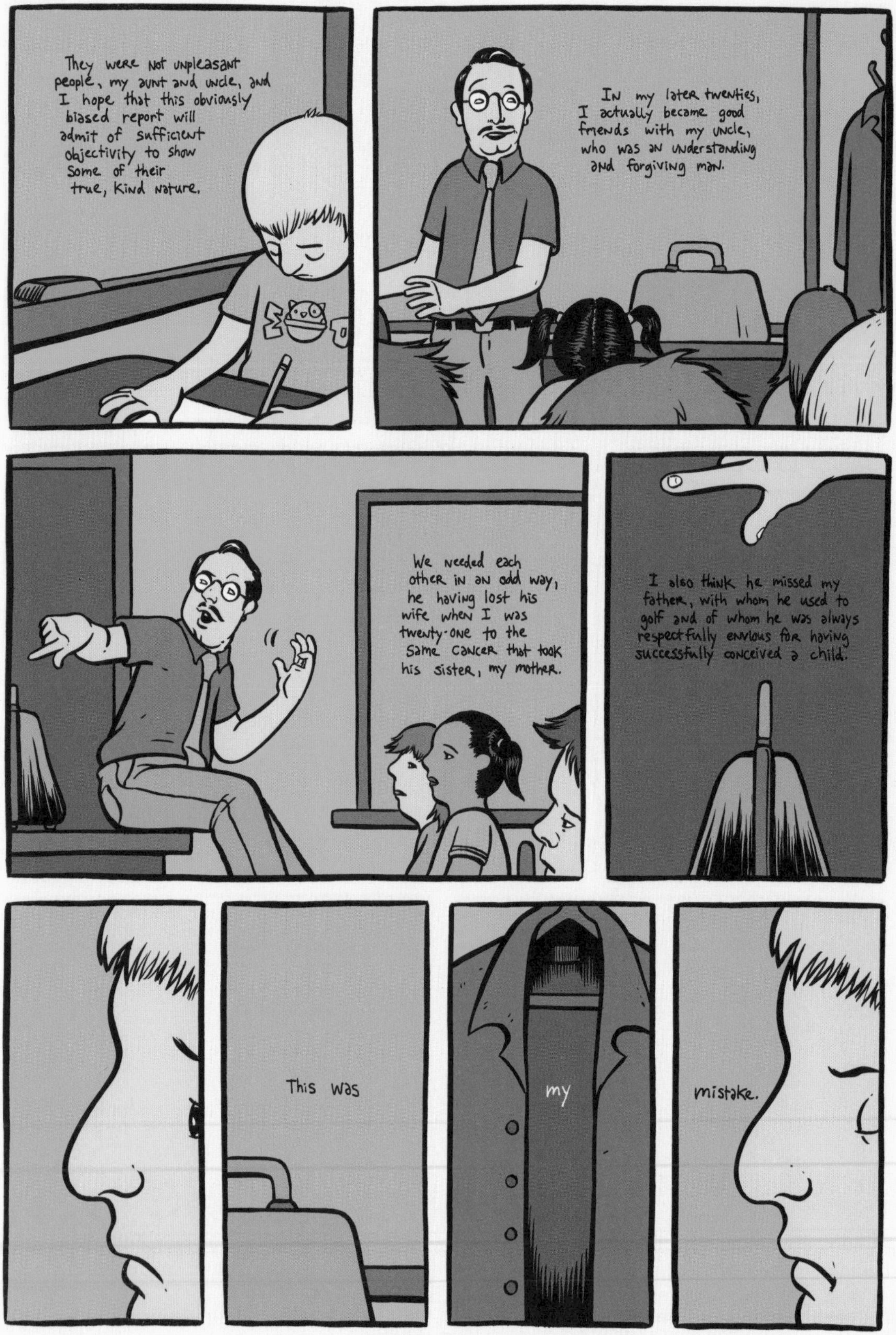
They were not unpleasant people, my aunt and uncle, and I hope that this obviously biased report will admit of sufficient objectivity to show some of their true, kind nature.
In my later twenties, I actually became good friends with my uncle, who was an understanding and forgiving man.
We needed each other in an odd way, he having lost his wife when I was twenty-one to the same cancer that took his sister, my mother.
I also think he missed my father, with whom he used to golf and of whom he was always respectfully envious for having successfully conceived a child.
This was
my
mistake.

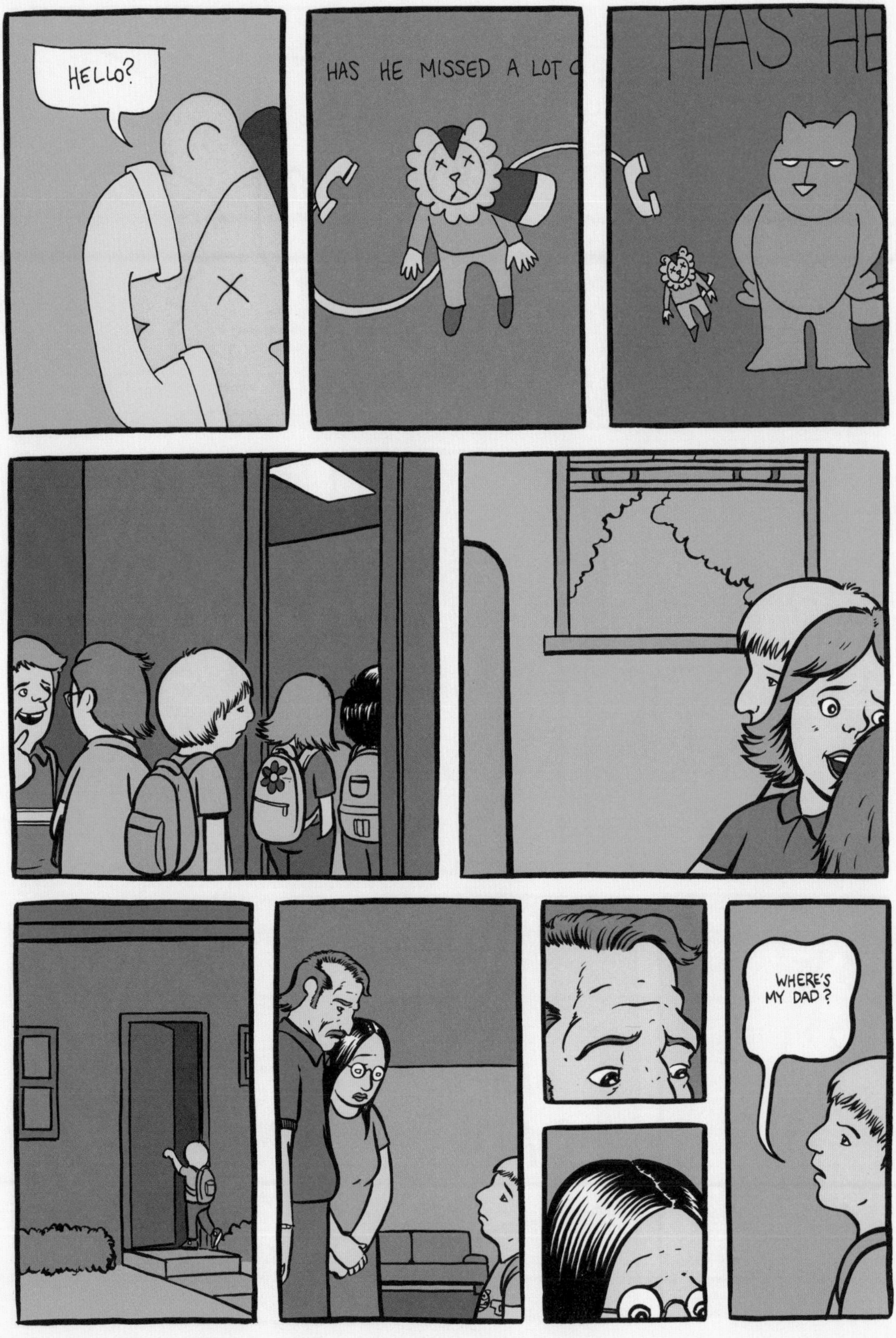
HELLO?
HAS HE MISSED A LOT
HAS HE
WHERE'S MY DAD?

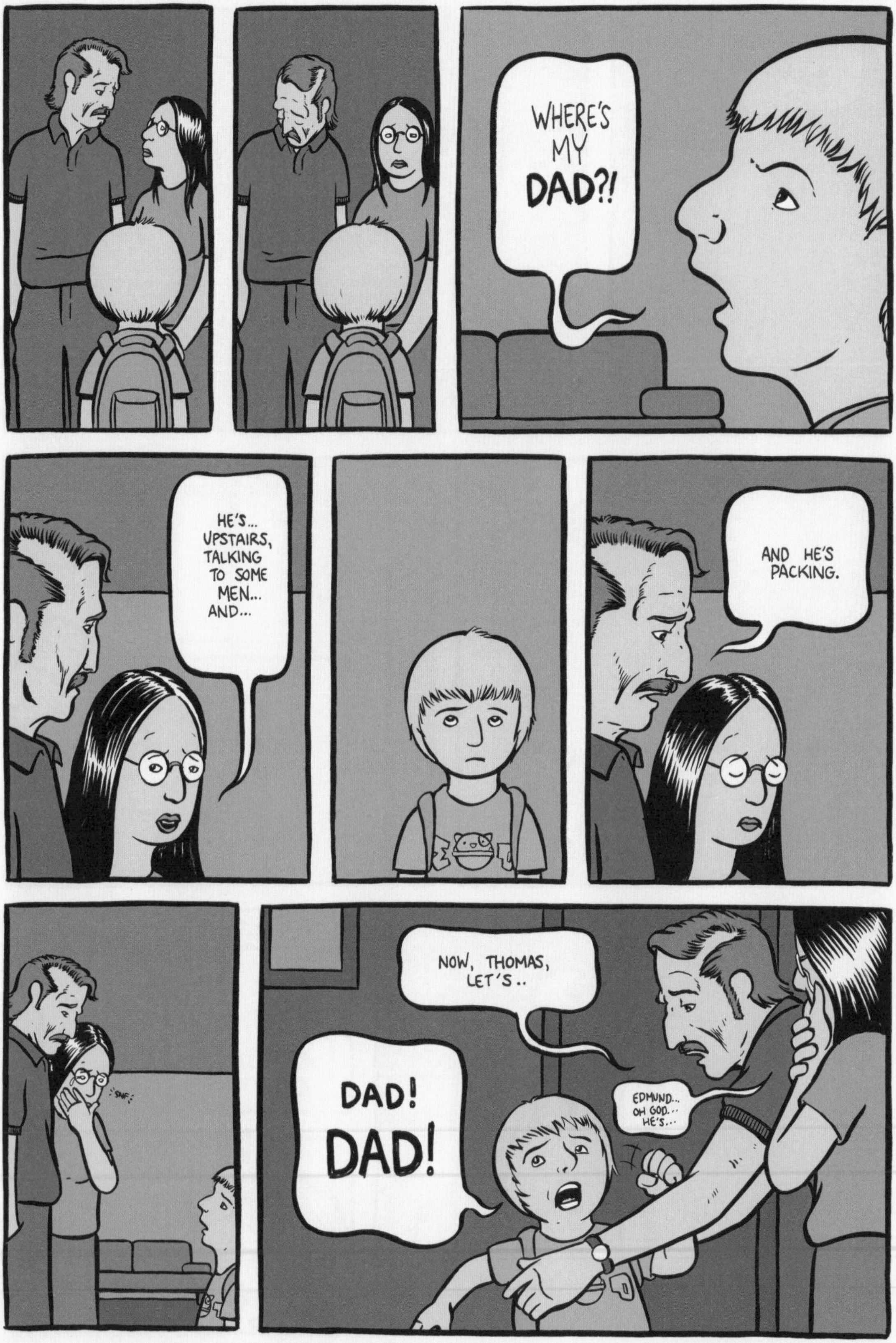
WHERE'S MY DAD?!
HE'S... UPSTAIRS, TALKING TO SOME MEN... AND...
AND HE'S PACKING.
SNF
NOW, THOMAS, LET'S..
DAD! DAD!
EDMUND... OH GOD... HE'S...

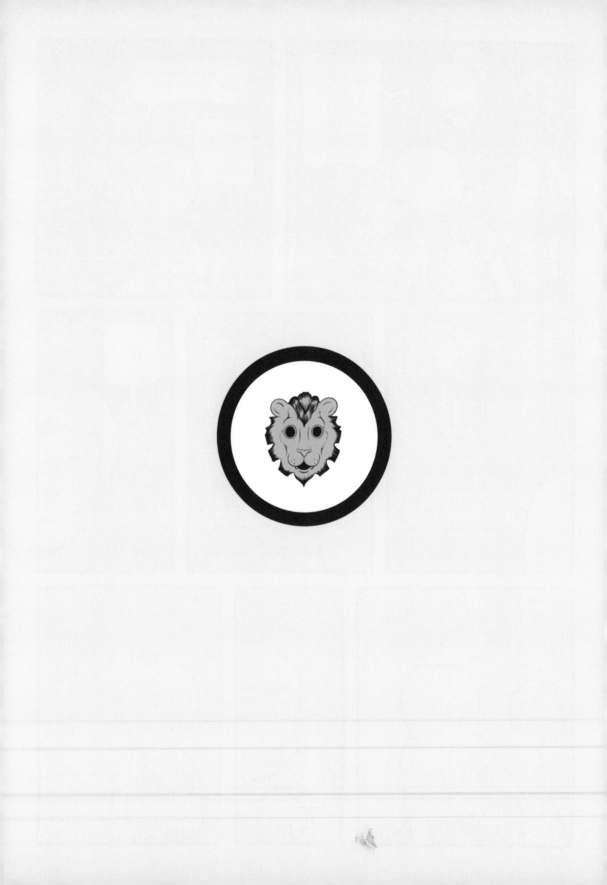

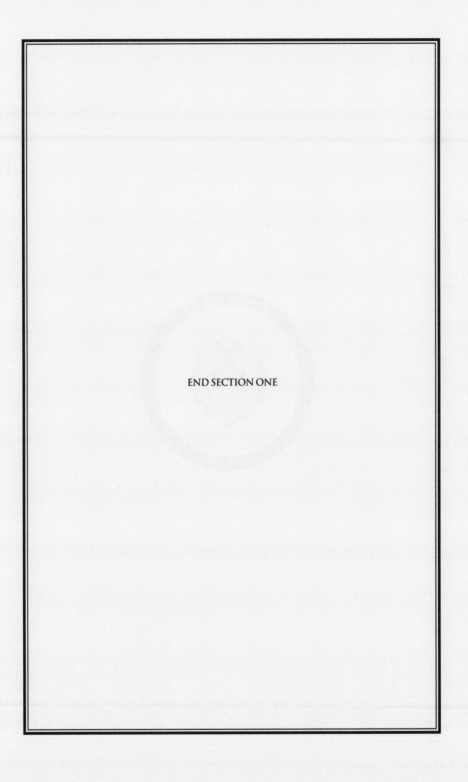

END SECTION ONE

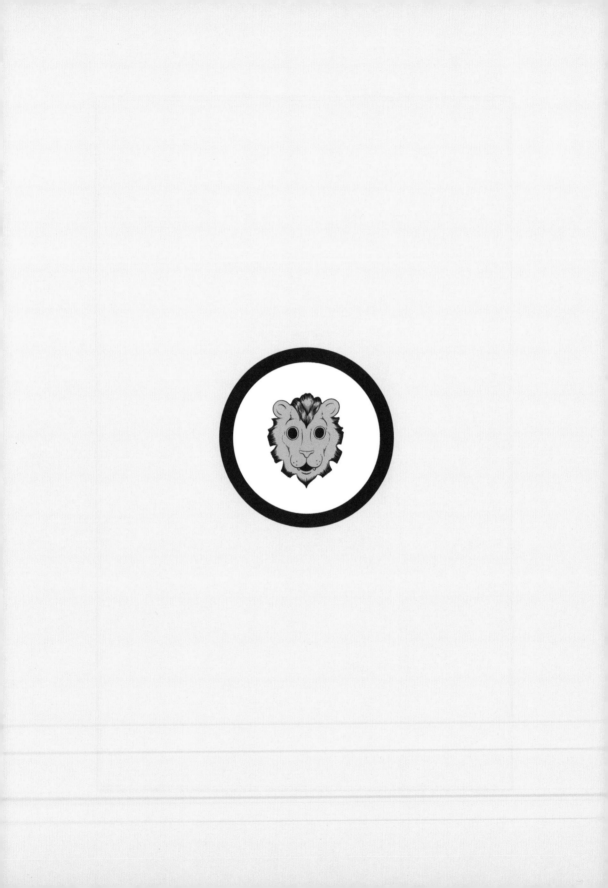

SECTION TWO:
"THE MEN FOR FATHER"

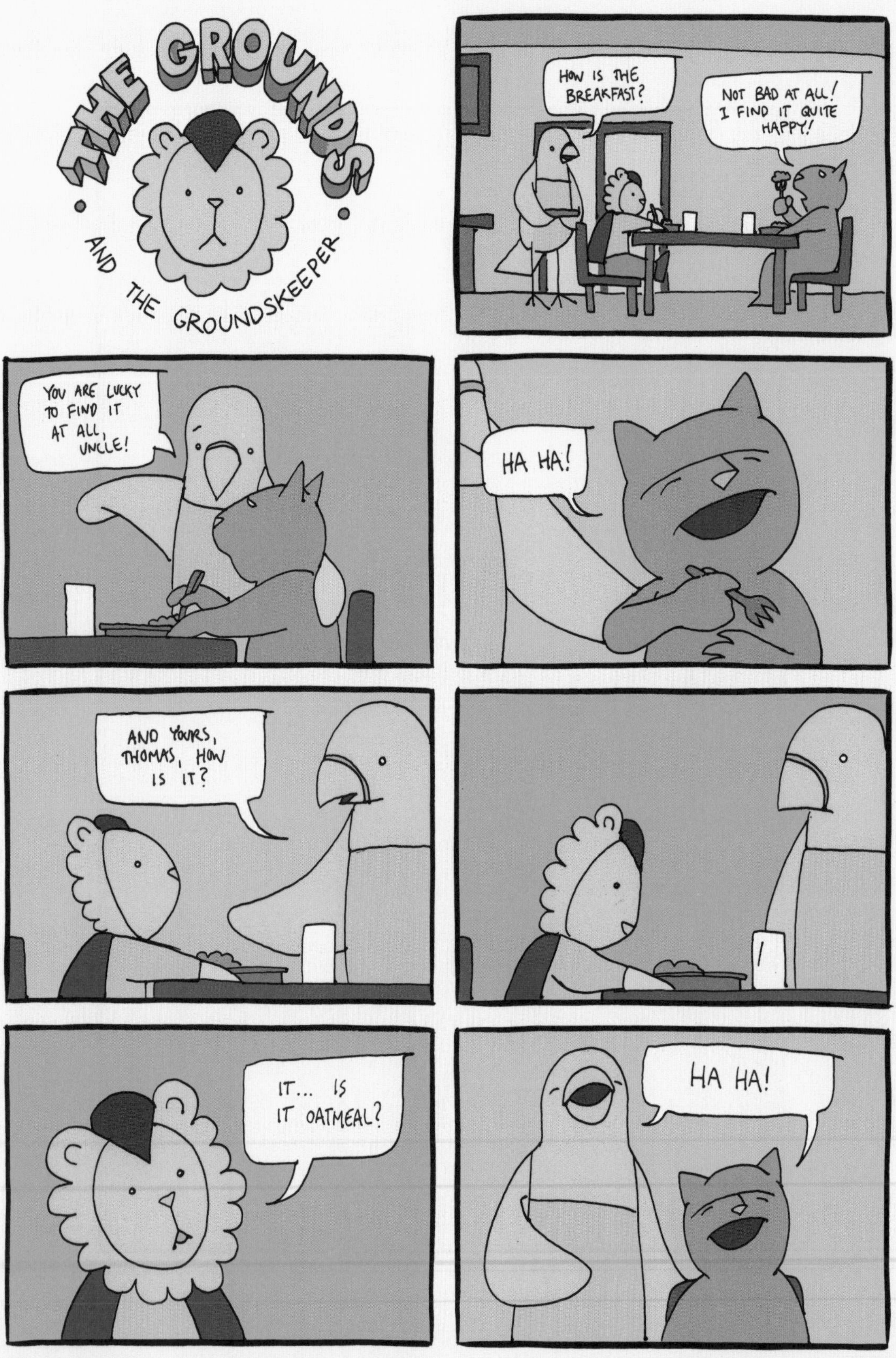
THE GROUNDS
AND THE GROUNDSKEEPER
HOW IS THE BREAKFAST?
NOT BAD AT ALL! I FIND IT QUITE HAPPY!
YOU ARE LUCKY TO FIND IT AT ALL, UNCLE!
HA HA!
AND YOURS, THOMAS, HOW IS IT?
IT... IS IT OATMEAL?
HA HA!

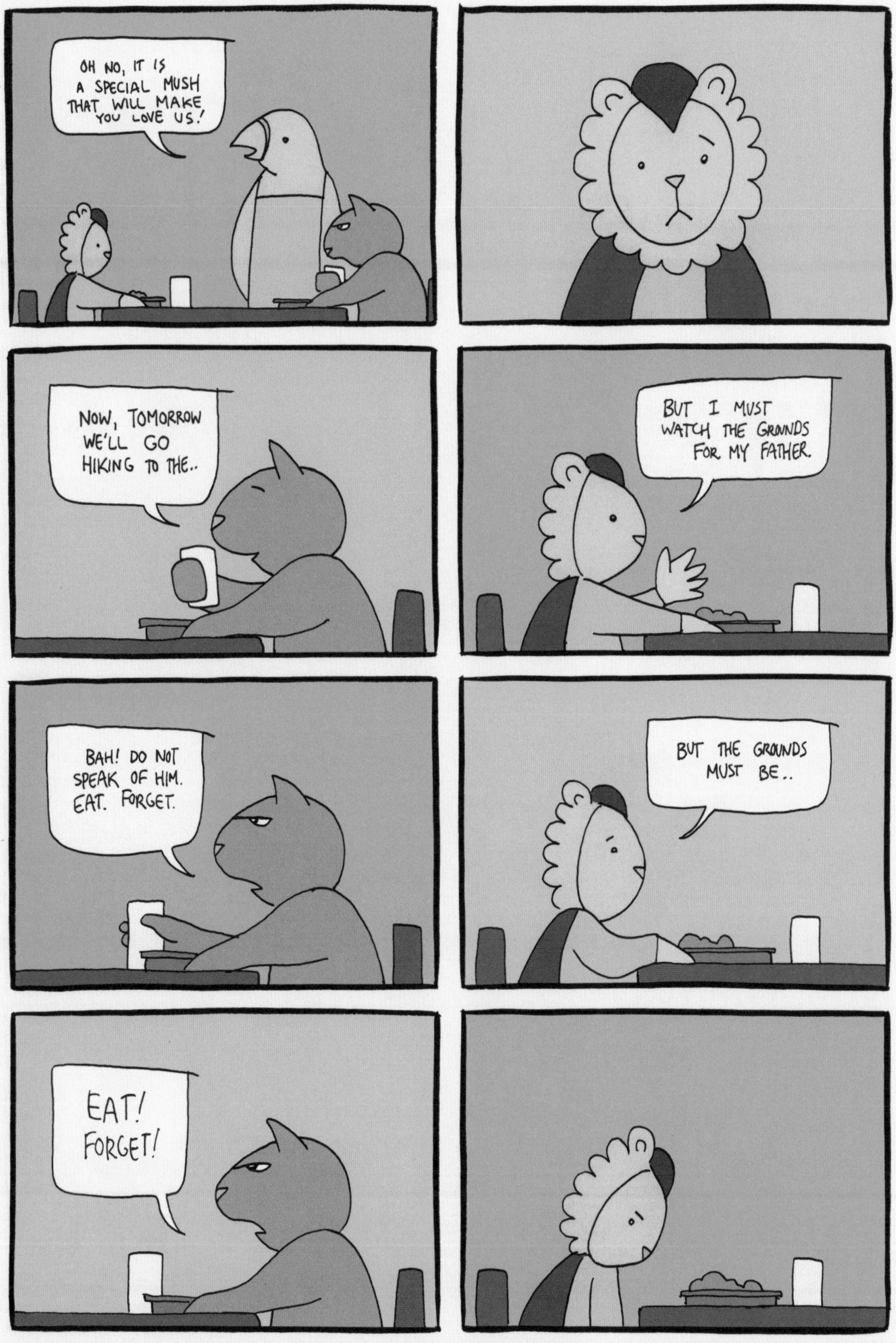
OH NO, IT IS A SPECIAL MUSH THAT WILL MAKE YOU LOVE US!
NOW, TOMORROW WE'LL GO HIKING TO THE..
BUT I MUST WATCH THE GROUNDS FOR MY FATHER.
BAH! DO NOT SPEAK OF HIM. EAT. FORGET.
BUT THE GROUNDS MUST BE..
EAT! FORGET!

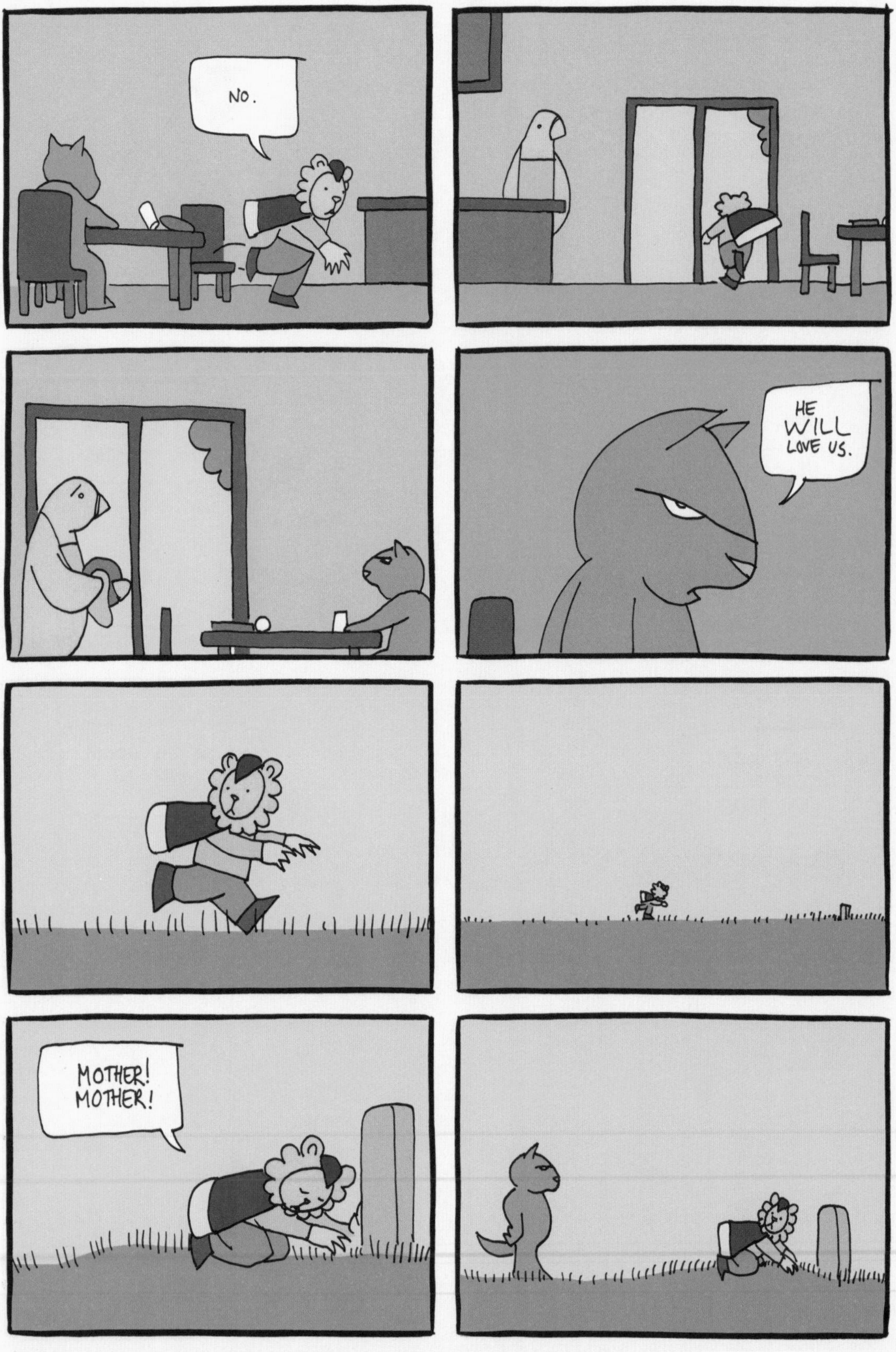
NO.
HE WILL LOVE US.
MOTHER! MOTHER!

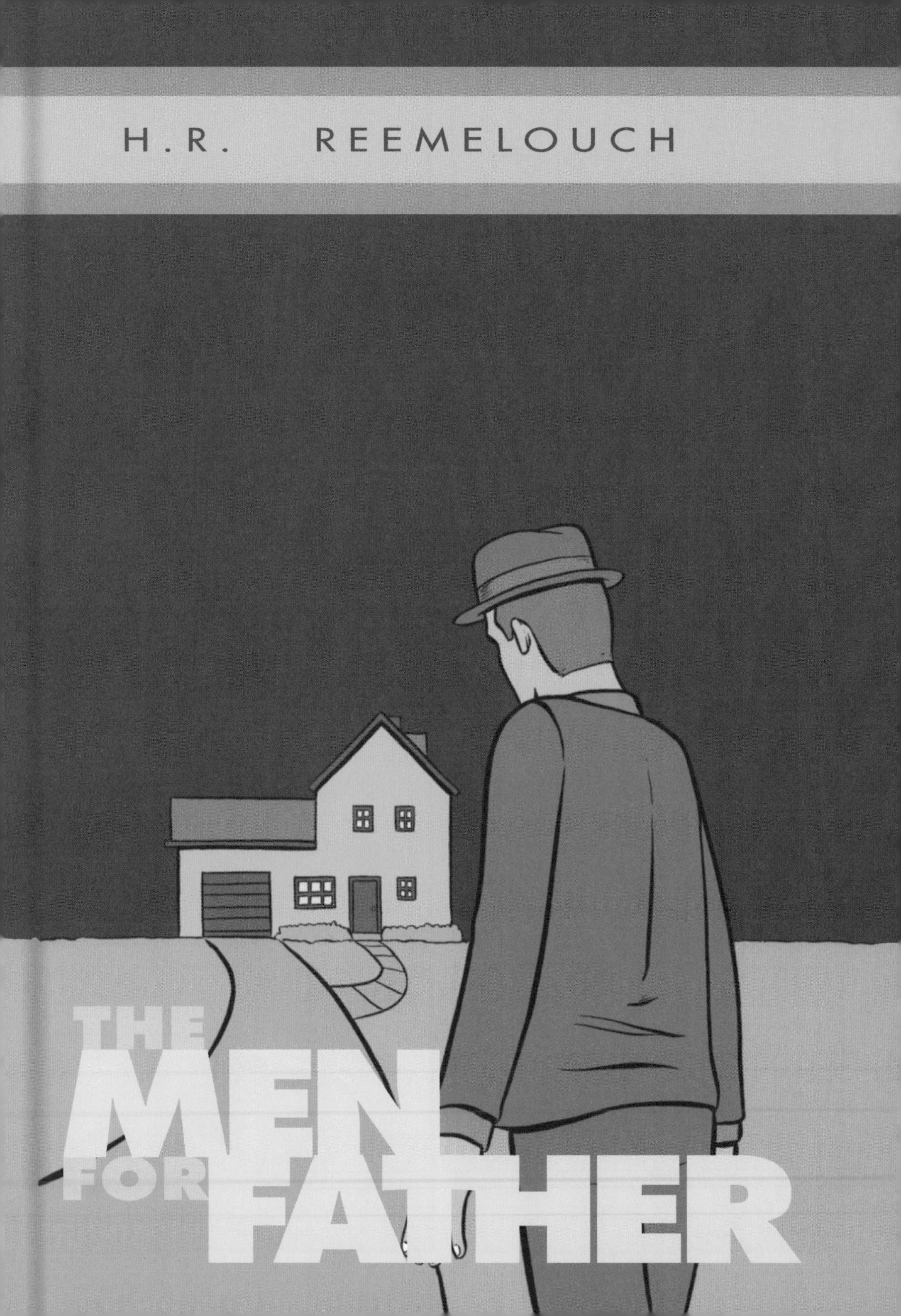
H.R. REEMELOUCH
THE MEN FOR FATHER

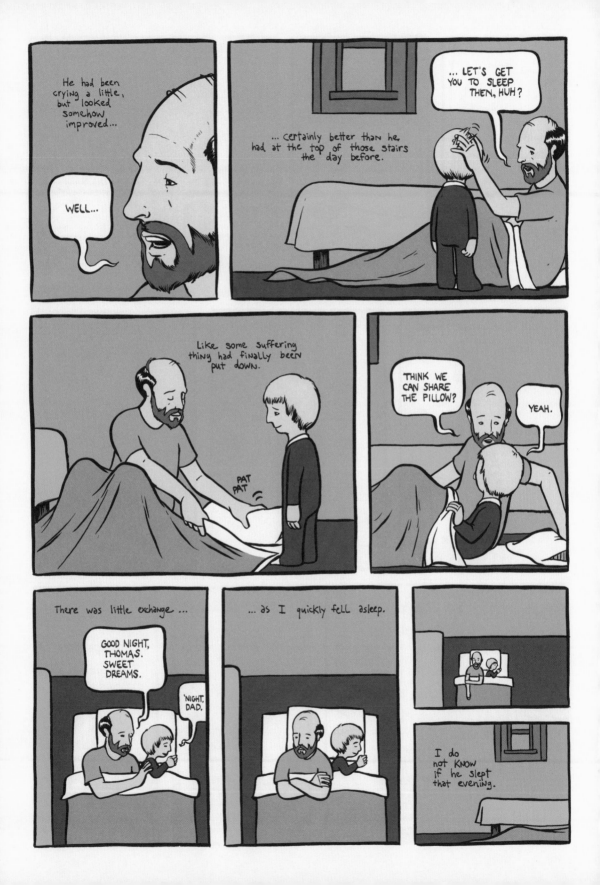

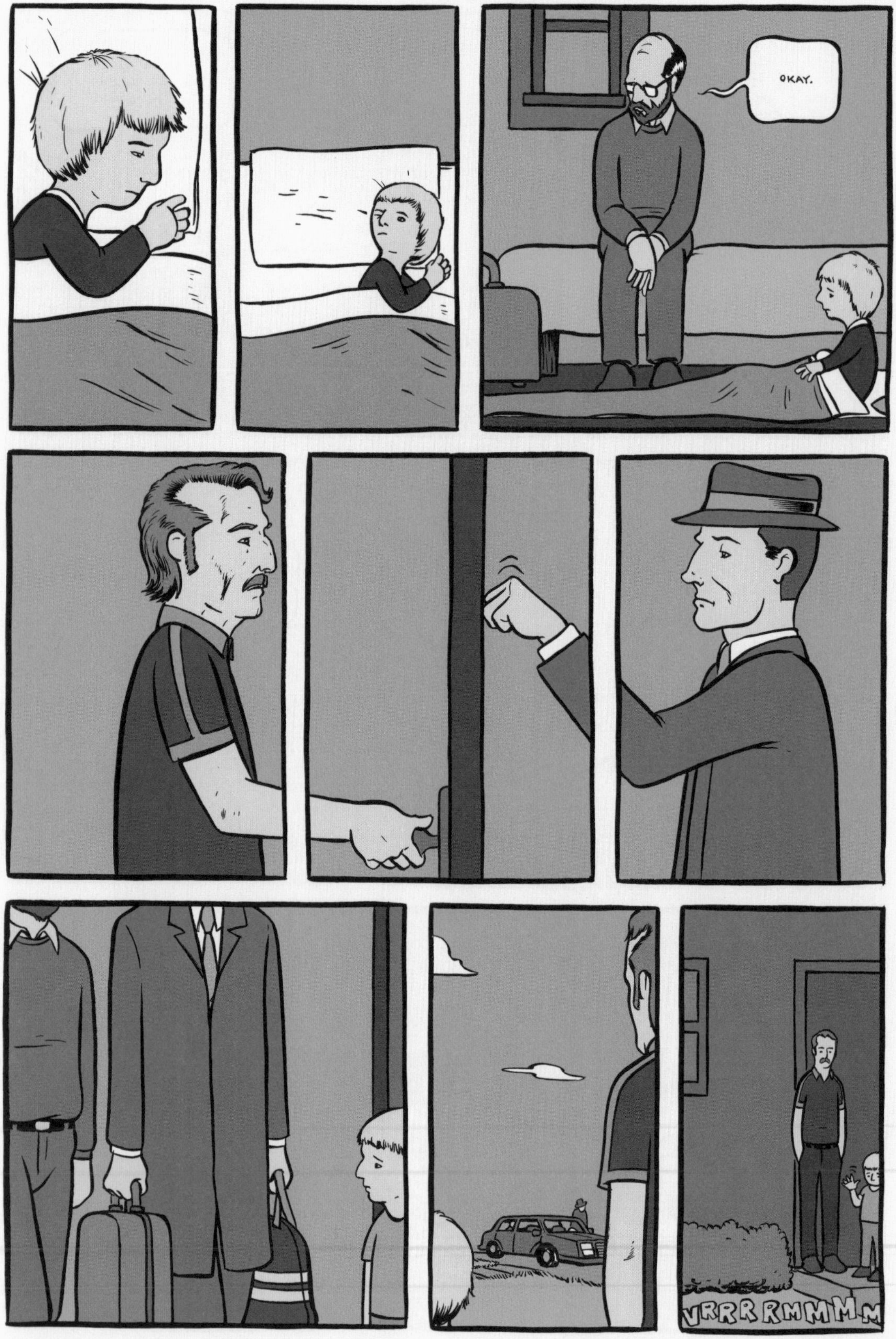
OKAY.
VRRRRMMMMM

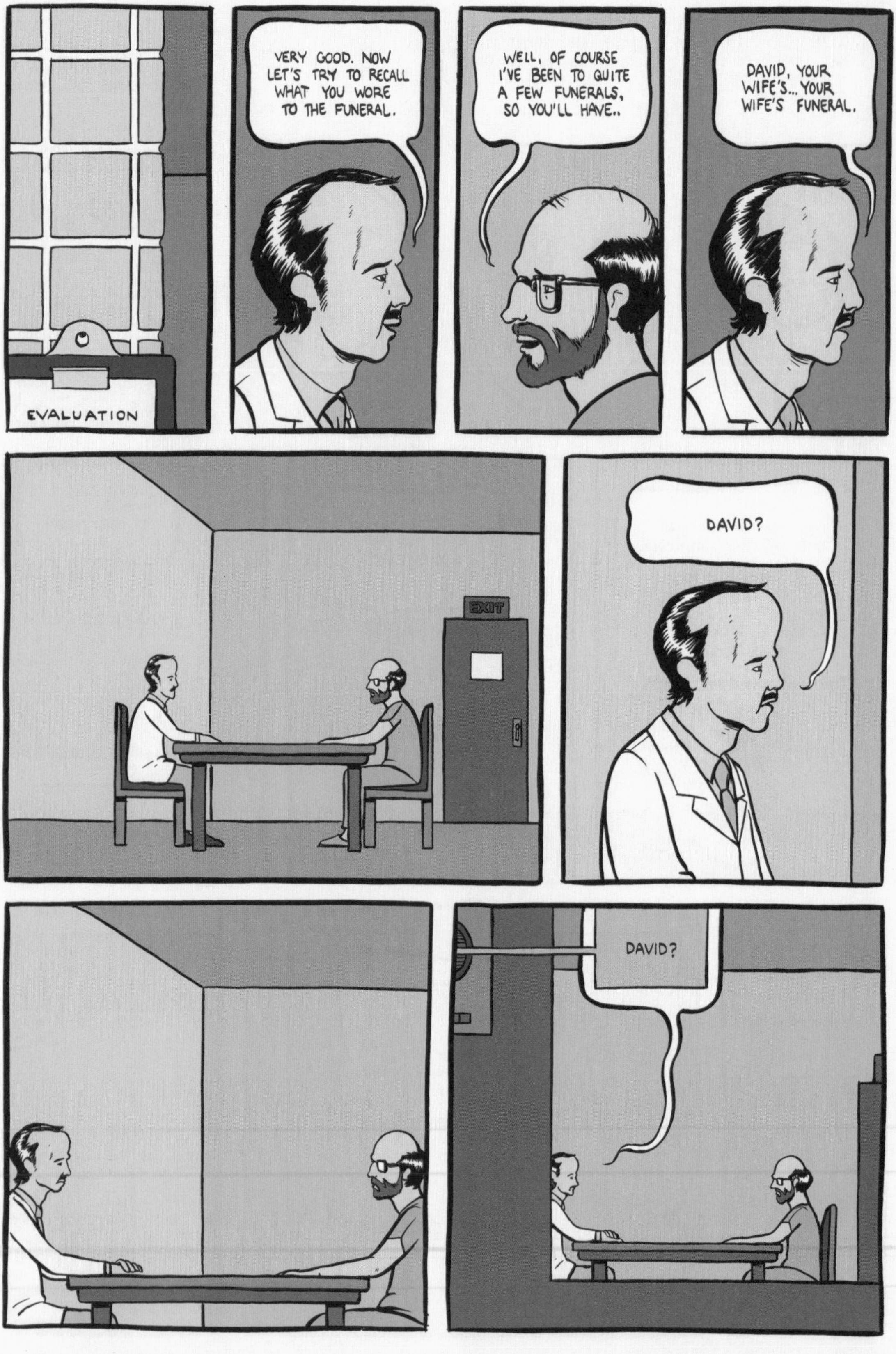
EVALUATION
VERY GOOD. NOW LET'S TRY TO RECALL WHAT YOU WORE TO THE FUNERAL.
WELL, OF COURSE I'VE BEEN TO QUITE A FEW FUNERALS, SO YOU'LL HAVE..
DAVID, YOUR WIFE'S... YOUR WIFE'S FUNERAL.
EXIT
DAVID?
DAVID?

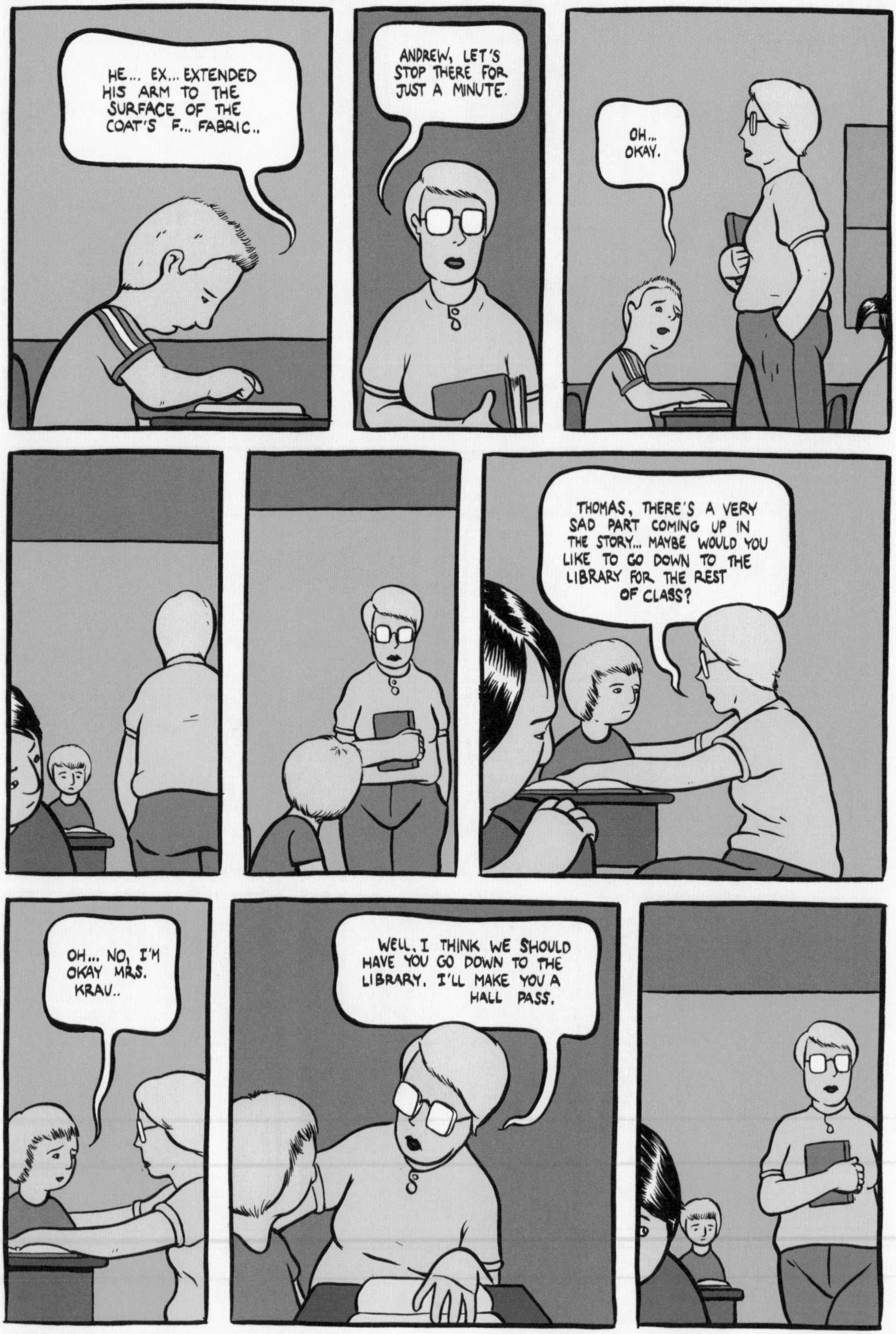
HE... EX... EXTENDED HIS ARM TO THE SURFACE OF THE COAT'S F... FABRIC..
ANDREW, LET'S STOP THERE FOR JUST A MINUTE.
OH... OKAY.
THOMAS, THERE'S A VERY SAD PART COMING UP IN THE STORY... MAYBE WOULD YOU LIKE TO GO DOWN TO THE LIBRARY FOR THE REST OF CLASS?
OH... NO, I'M OKAY MRS. KRAU..
WELL, I THINK WE SHOULD HAVE YOU GO DOWN TO THE LIBRARY. I'LL MAKE YOU A HALL PASS.

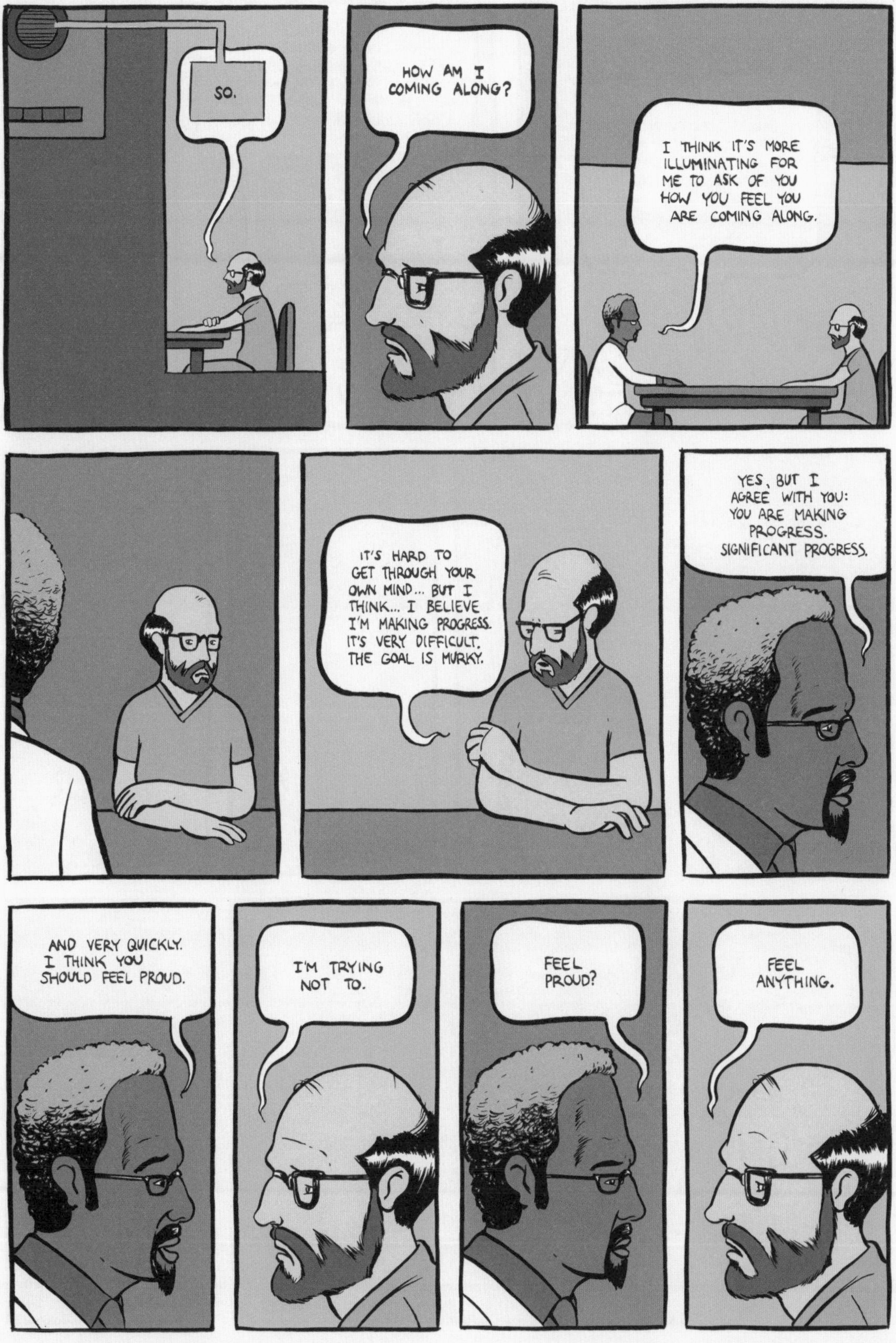
SO.
HOW AM I COMING ALONG?
I THINK IT'S MORE ILLUMINATING FOR ME TO ASK OF YOU HOW YOU FEEL YOU ARE COMING ALONG.
IT'S HARD TO GET THROUGH YOUR OWN MIND... BUT I THINK... I BELIEVE I'M MAKING PROGRESS. IT'S VERY DIFFICULT. THE GOAL IS MURKY.
YES, BUT I AGREE WITH YOU: YOU ARE MAKING PROGRESS. SIGNIFICANT PROGRESS.
AND VERY QUICKLY. I THINK YOU SHOULD FEEL PROUD.
I'M TRYING NOT TO.
FEEL PROUD?
FEEL ANYTHING.

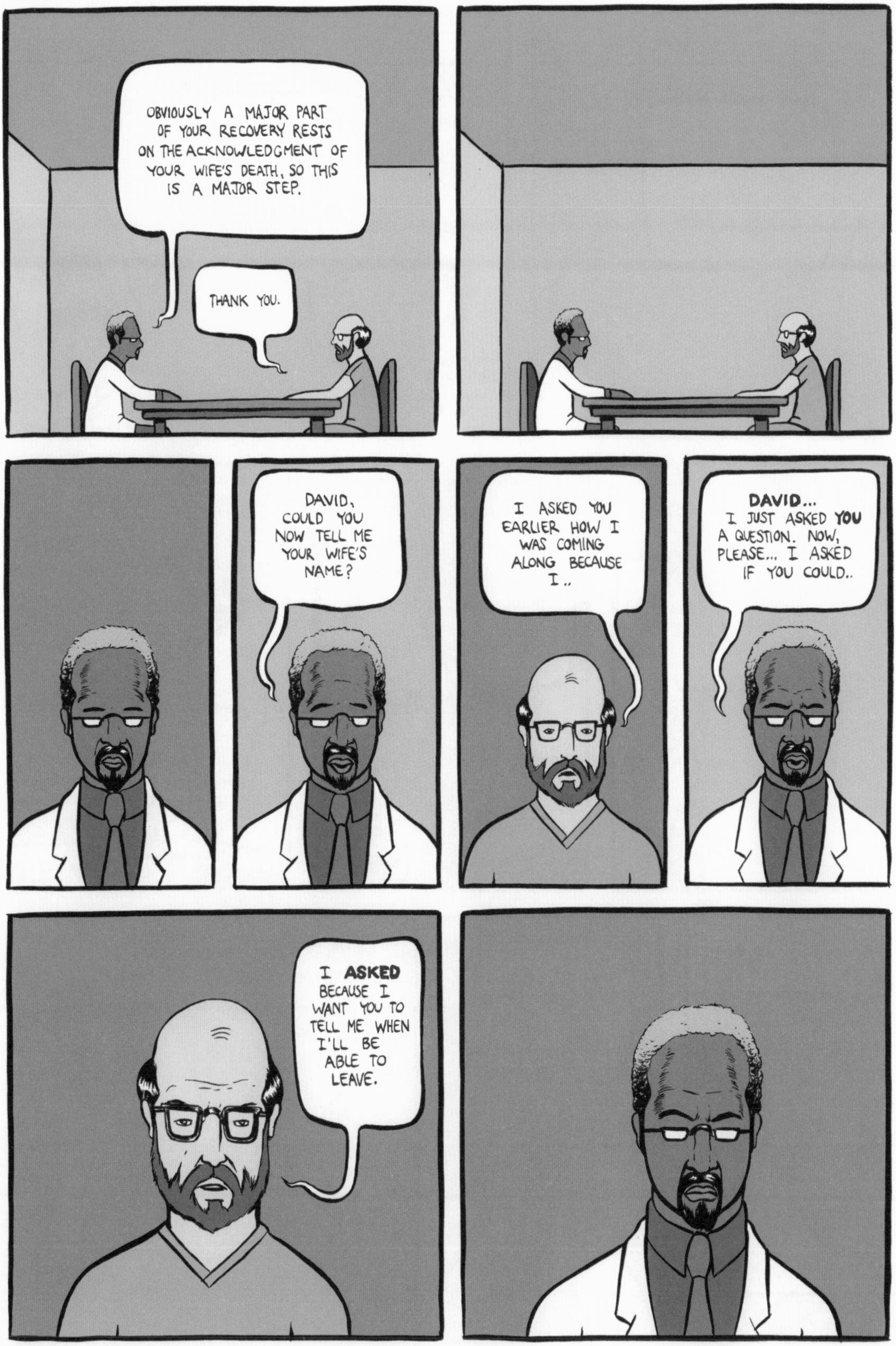
OBVIOUSLY A MAJOR PART OF YOUR RECOVERY RESTS ON THE ACKNOWLEDGMENT OF YOUR WIFE'S DEATH, SO THIS IS A MAJOR STEP.
THANK YOU.
DAVID, COULD YOU NOW TELL ME YOUR WIFE'S NAME?
I ASKED YOU EARLIER HOW I WAS COMING ALONG BECAUSE I..
DAVID... I JUST ASKED YOU A QUESTION. NOW, PLEASE... I ASKED IF YOU COULD..
I ASKED BECAUSE I WANT YOU TO TELL ME WHEN I'LL BE ABLE TO LEAVE.

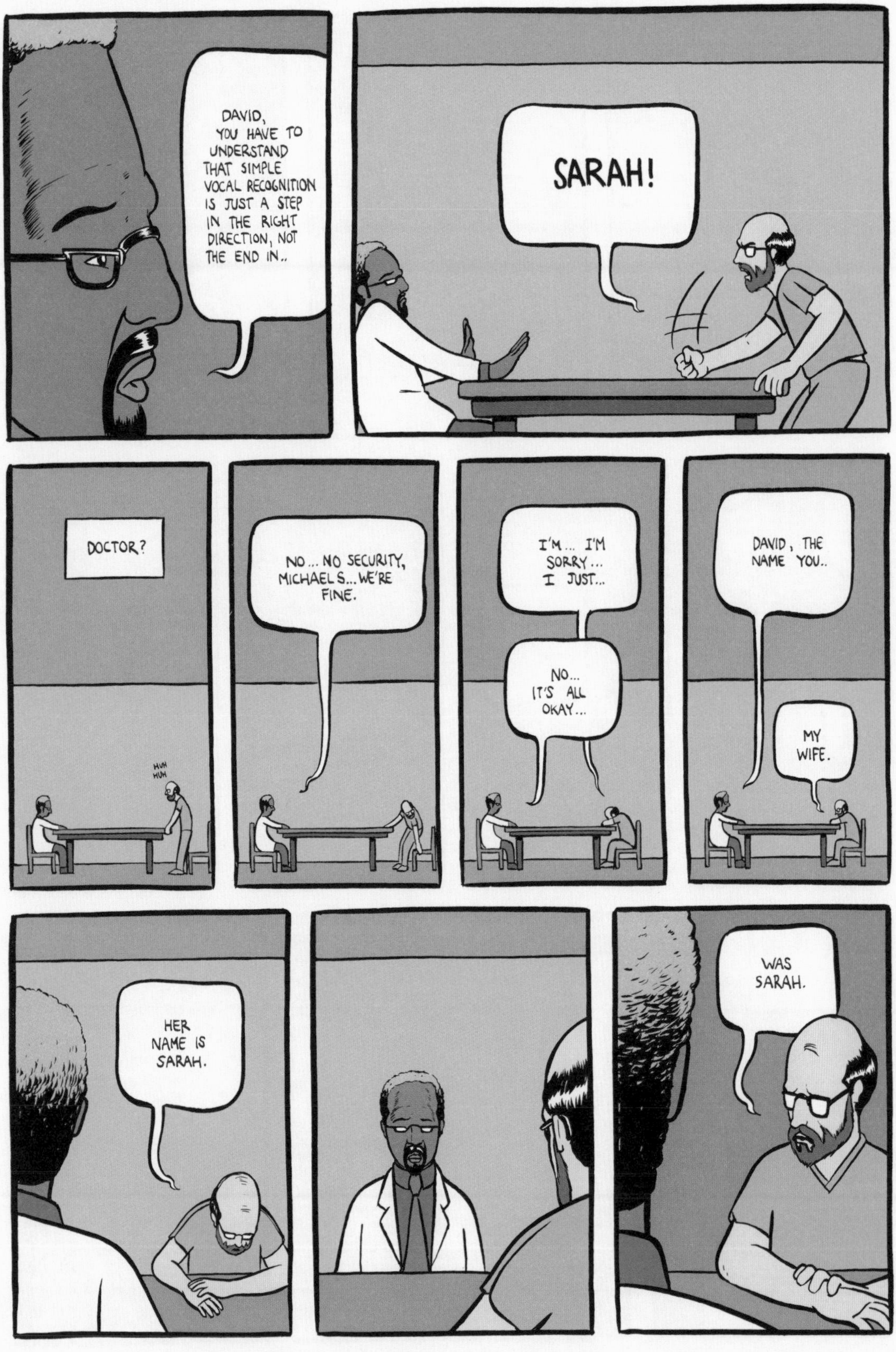
DAVID, YOU HAVE TO UNDERSTAND THAT SIMPLE VOCAL RECOGNITION IS JUST A STEP IN THE RIGHT DIRECTION, NOT THE END IN..
SARAH!
DOCTOR?
HUH HUH
NO... NO SECURITY, MICHAELS... WE'RE FINE.
I'M... I'M SORRY... I JUST...
NO... IT'S ALL OKAY...
DAVID, THE NAME YOU..
MY WIFE.
HER NAME IS SARAH.
WAS SARAH.

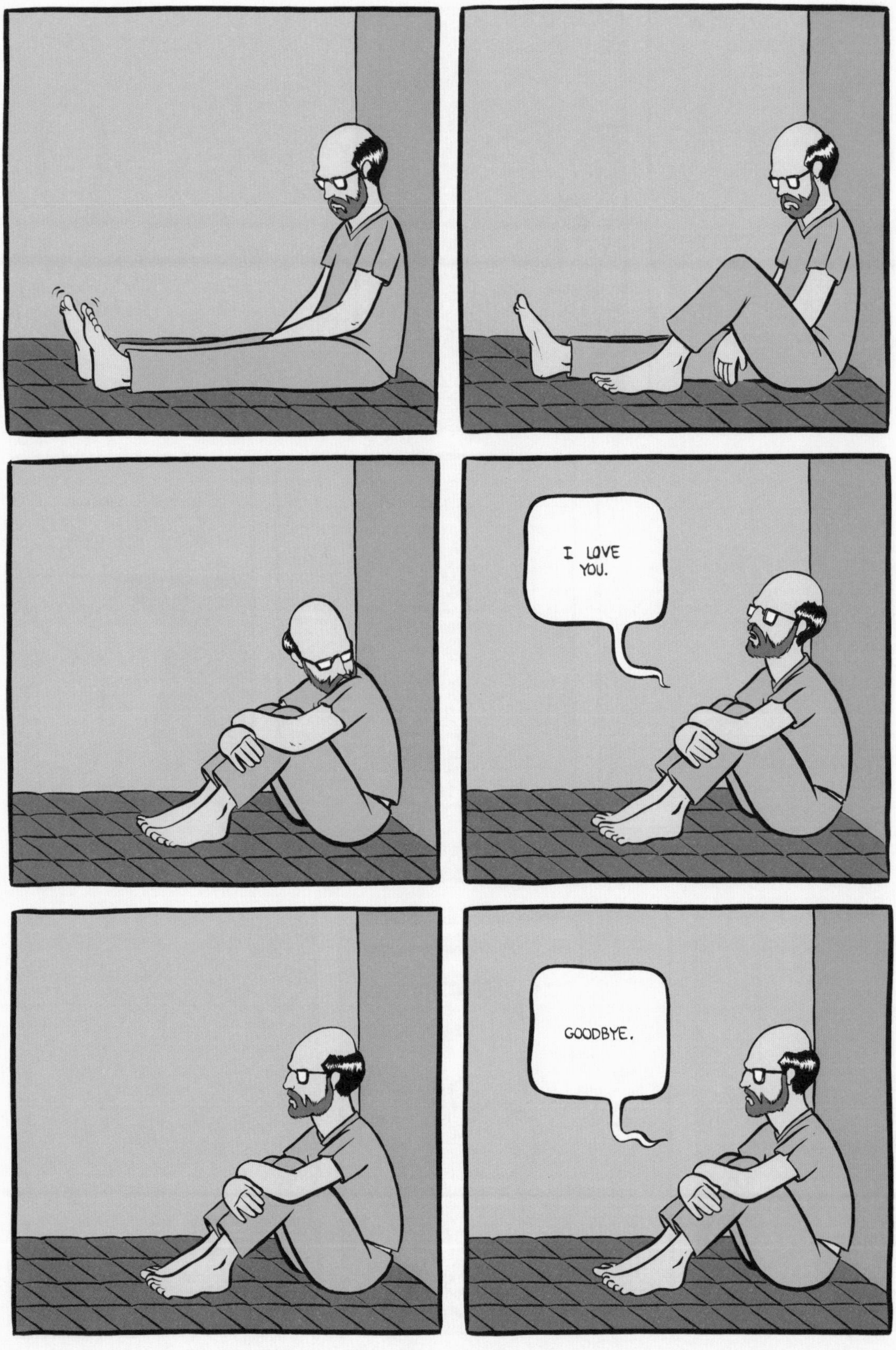
I LOVE YOU.
GOODBYE.

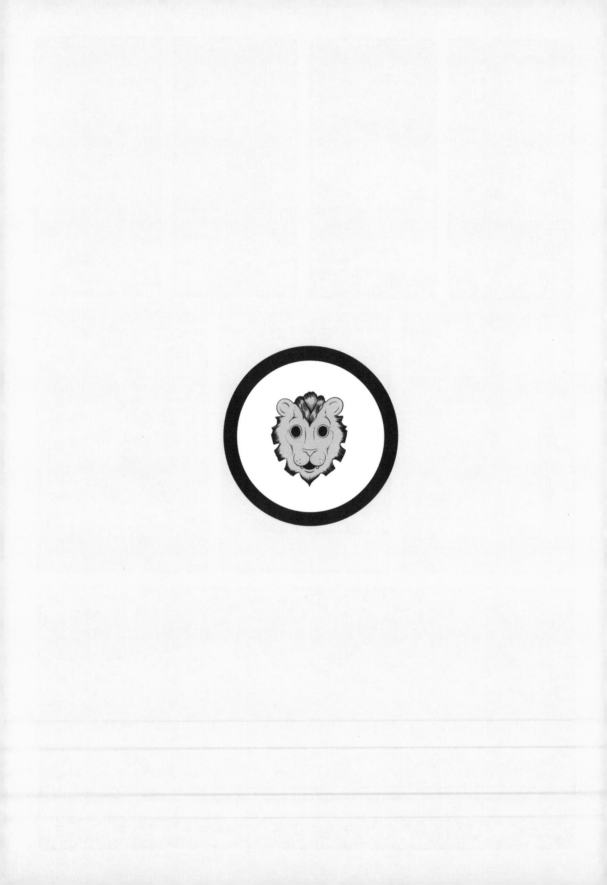

END SECTION TWO

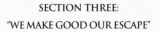

SECTION THREE:
"WE MAKE GOOD OUR ESCAPE"

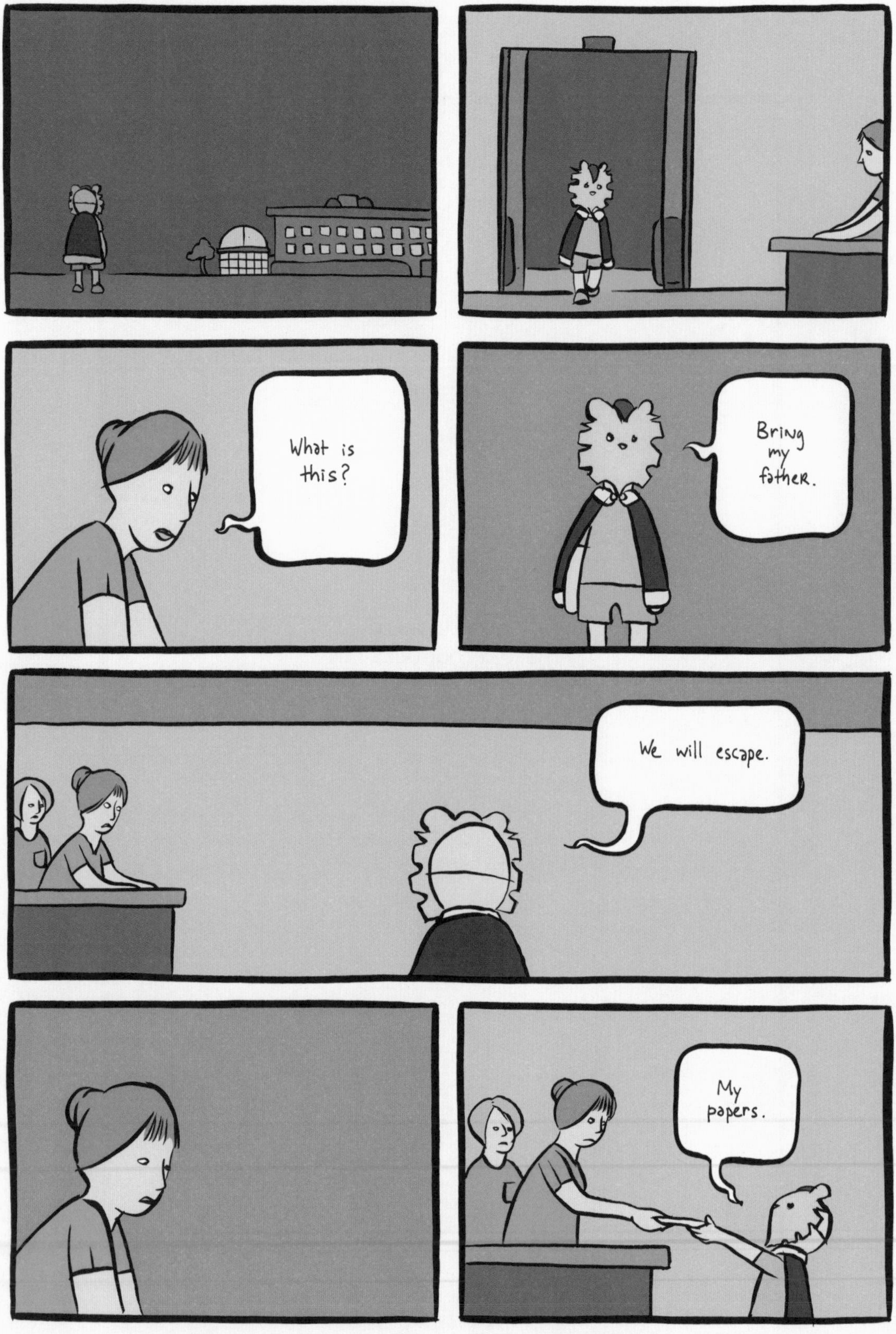
What is this?
Bring my father.
We will escape.
My papers.

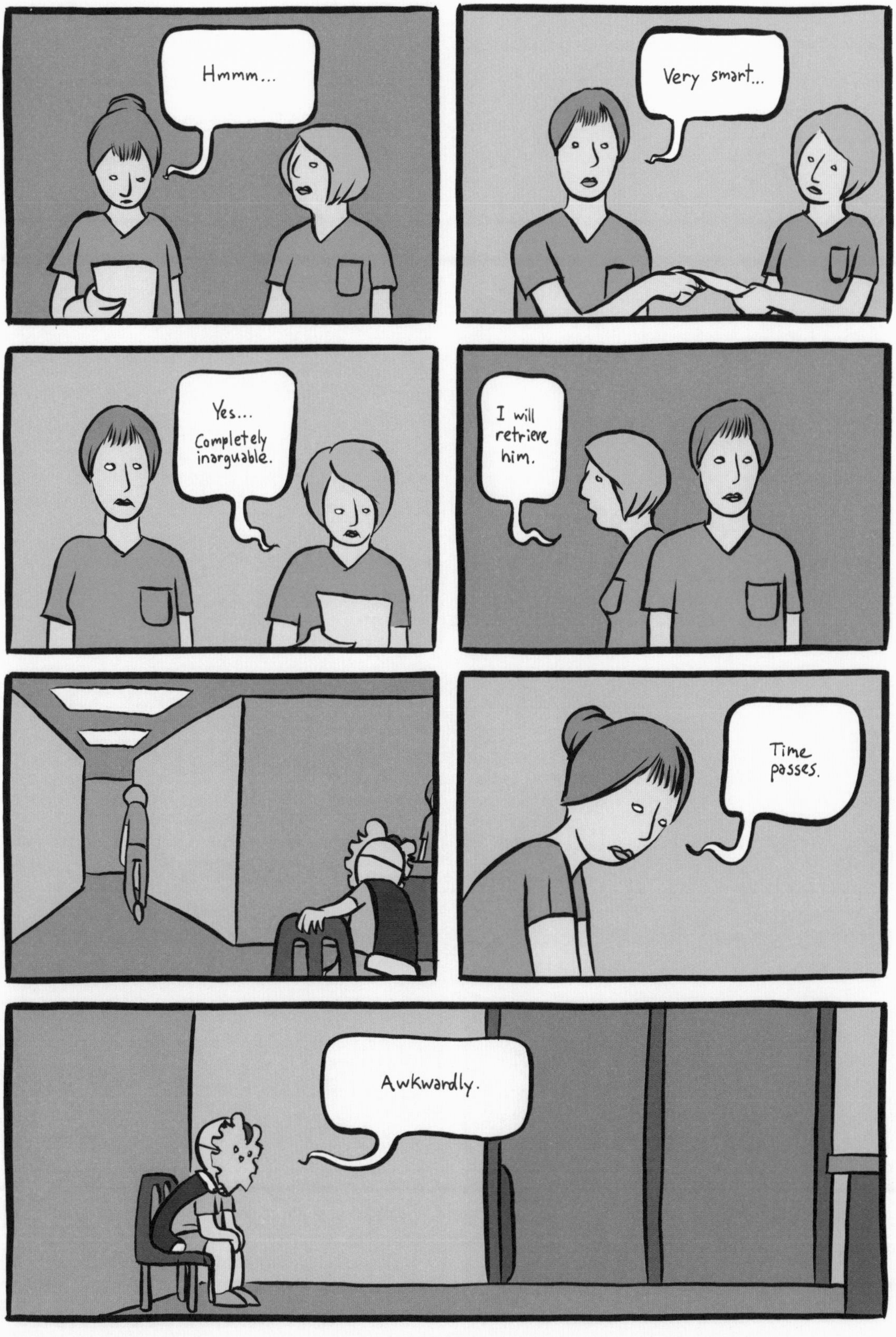
Hmmm...
Very smart...
Yes... Completely inarguable.
I will retrieve him.
Time passes.
Awkwardly.

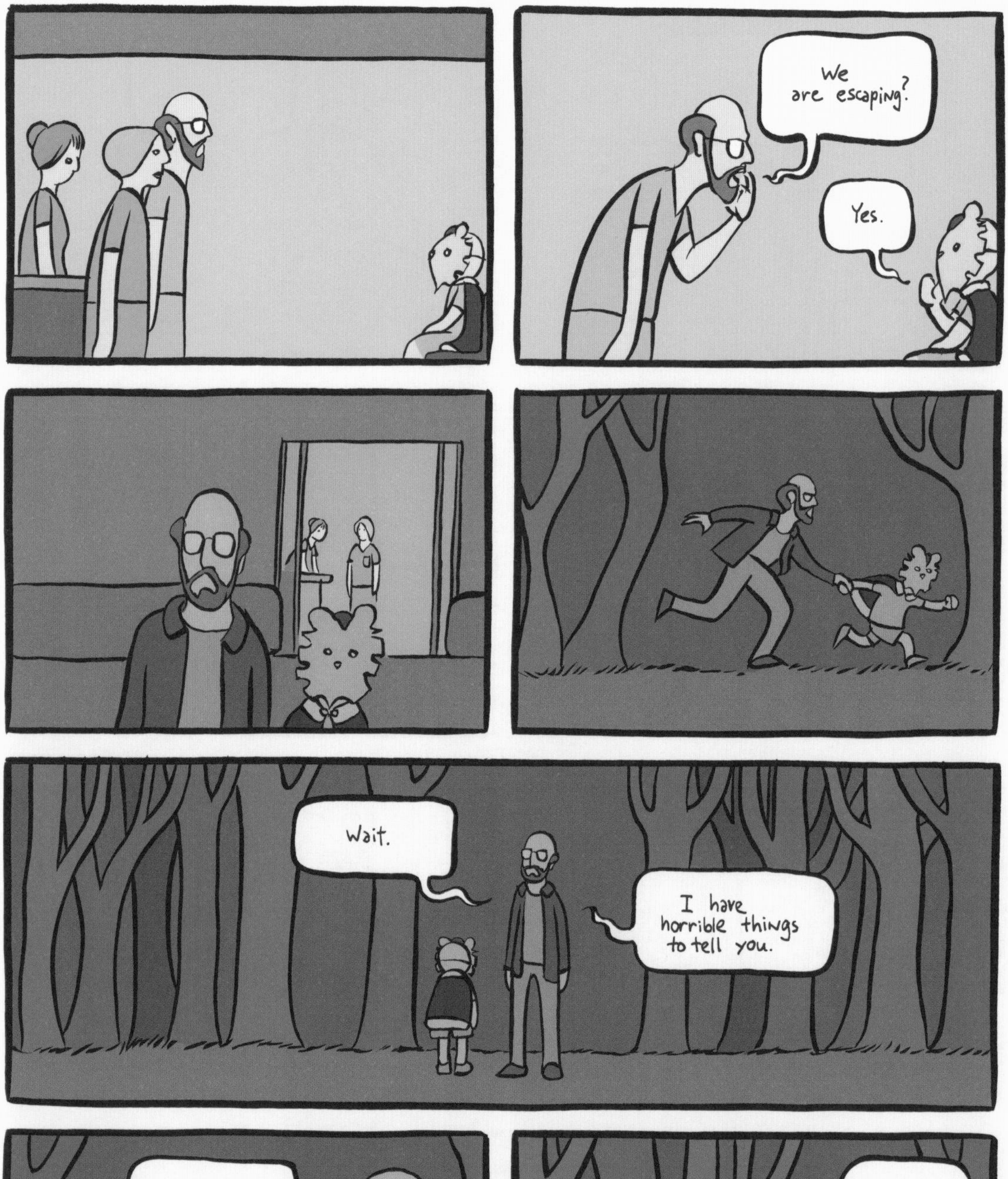
We are escaping?
Yes.
Wait.
I have horrible things to tell you.
Nothing is very simple.
Then we should keep running.

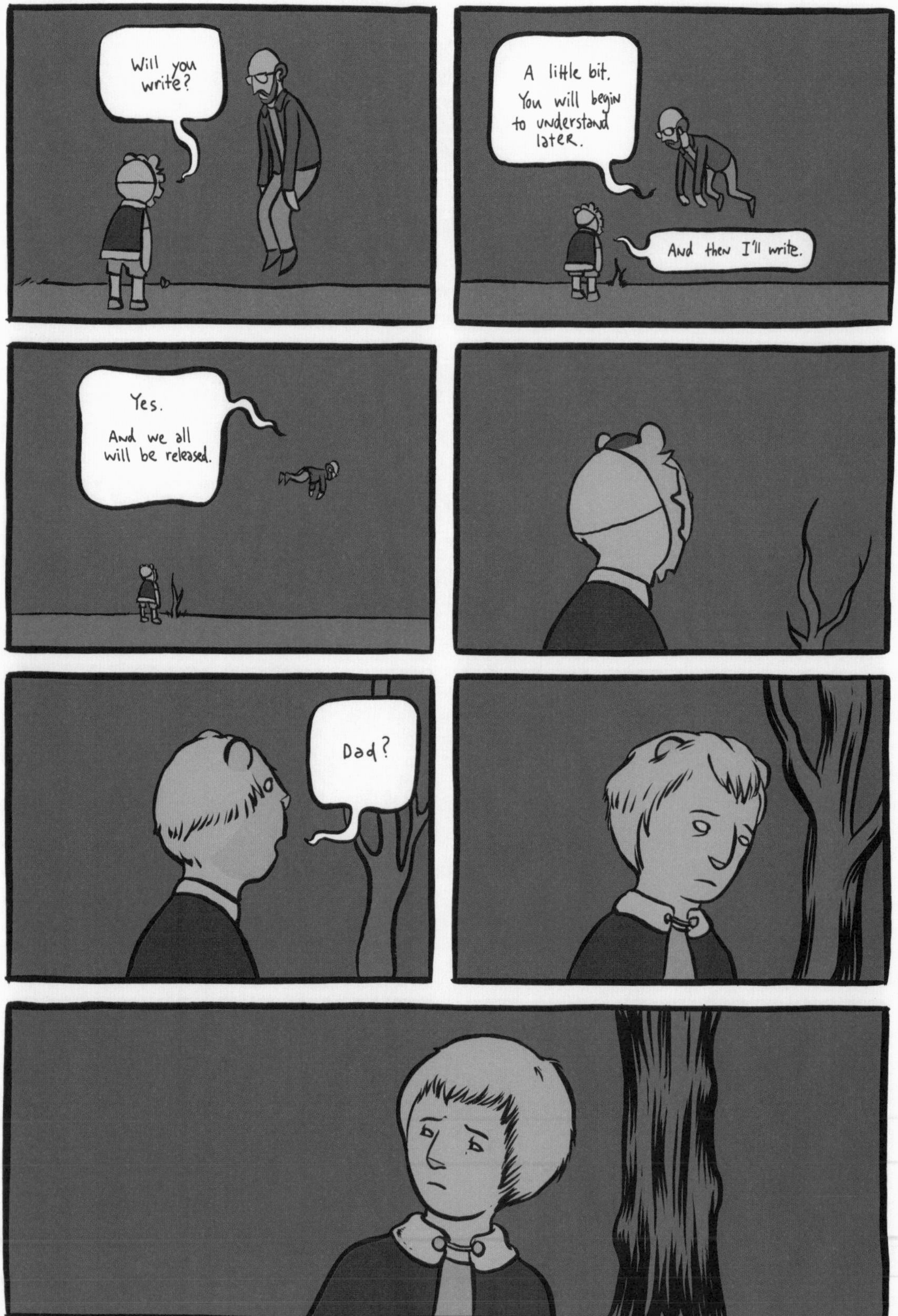
Will you write?
A little bit. You will begin to understand later.
And then I'll write.
Yes. And we all will be released.
Dad?

It took hours, and I can only imagine how tired my legs must have been.
I say this because I do not think, at the time, that I could feel anything.

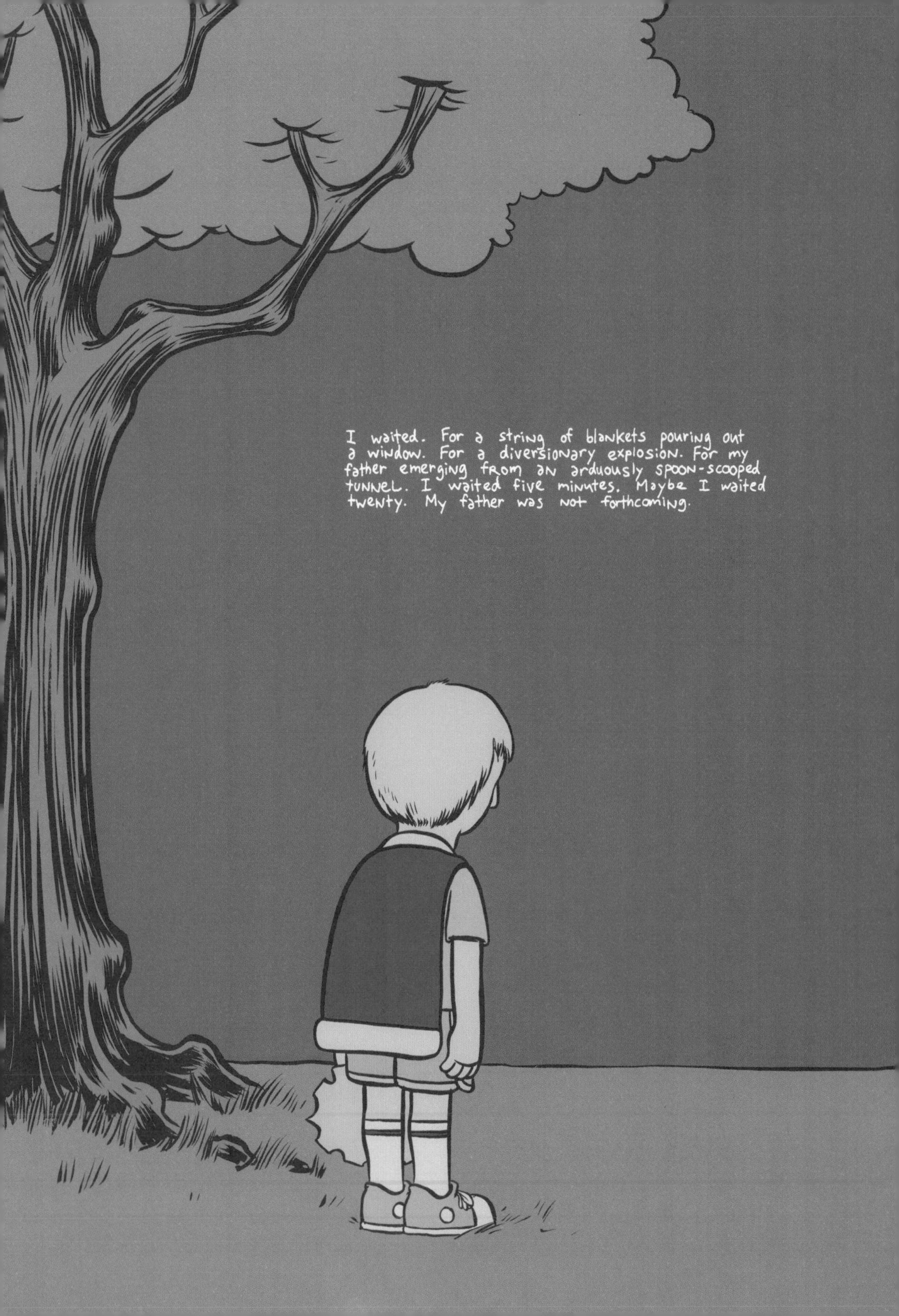
I waited. For a string of blankets pouring out a window. For a diversionary explosion. For my father emerging from an arduously spoon-scooped tunnel. I waited five minutes. Maybe I waited twenty. My father was not forthcoming.

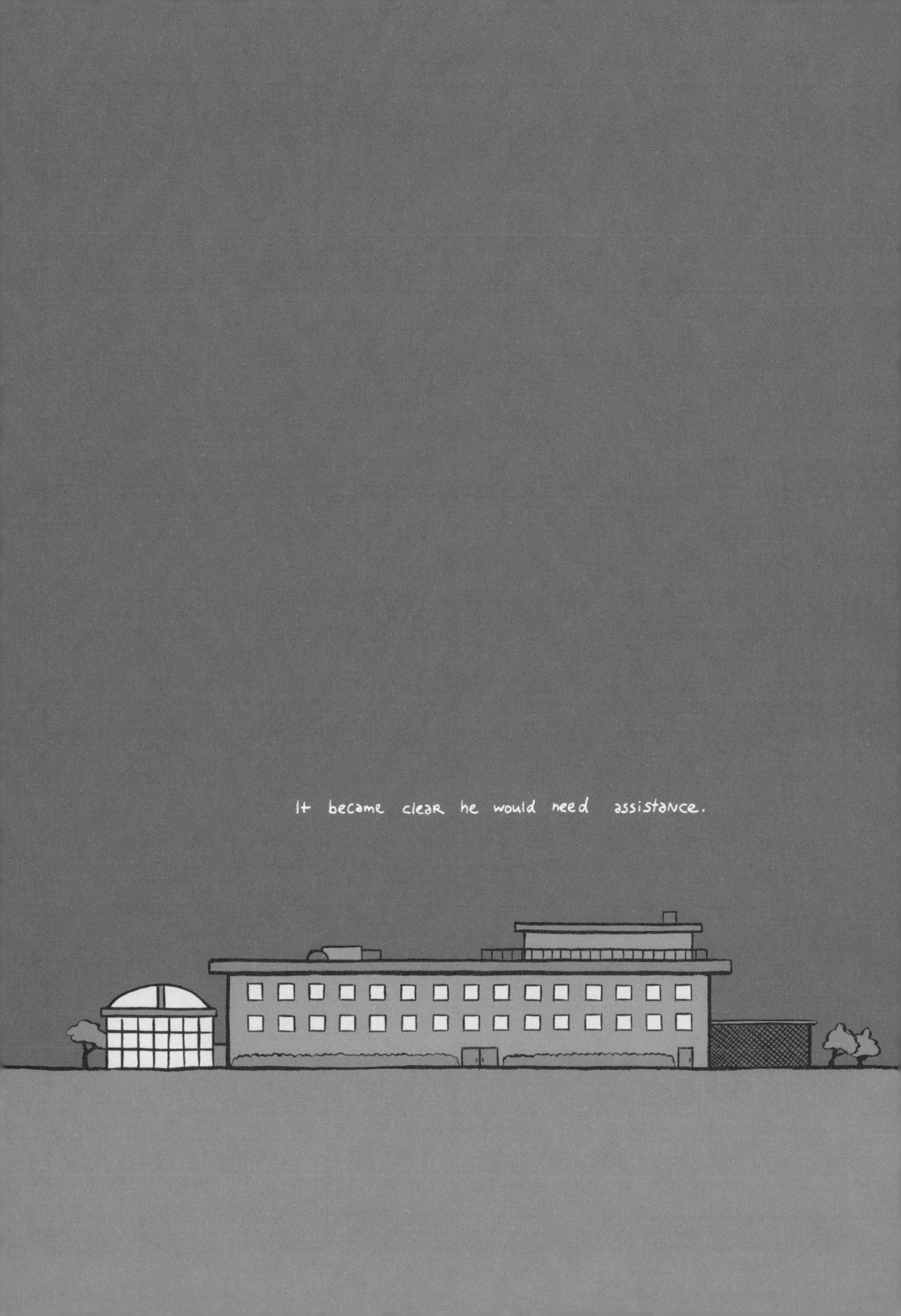
It became clear he would need assistance.

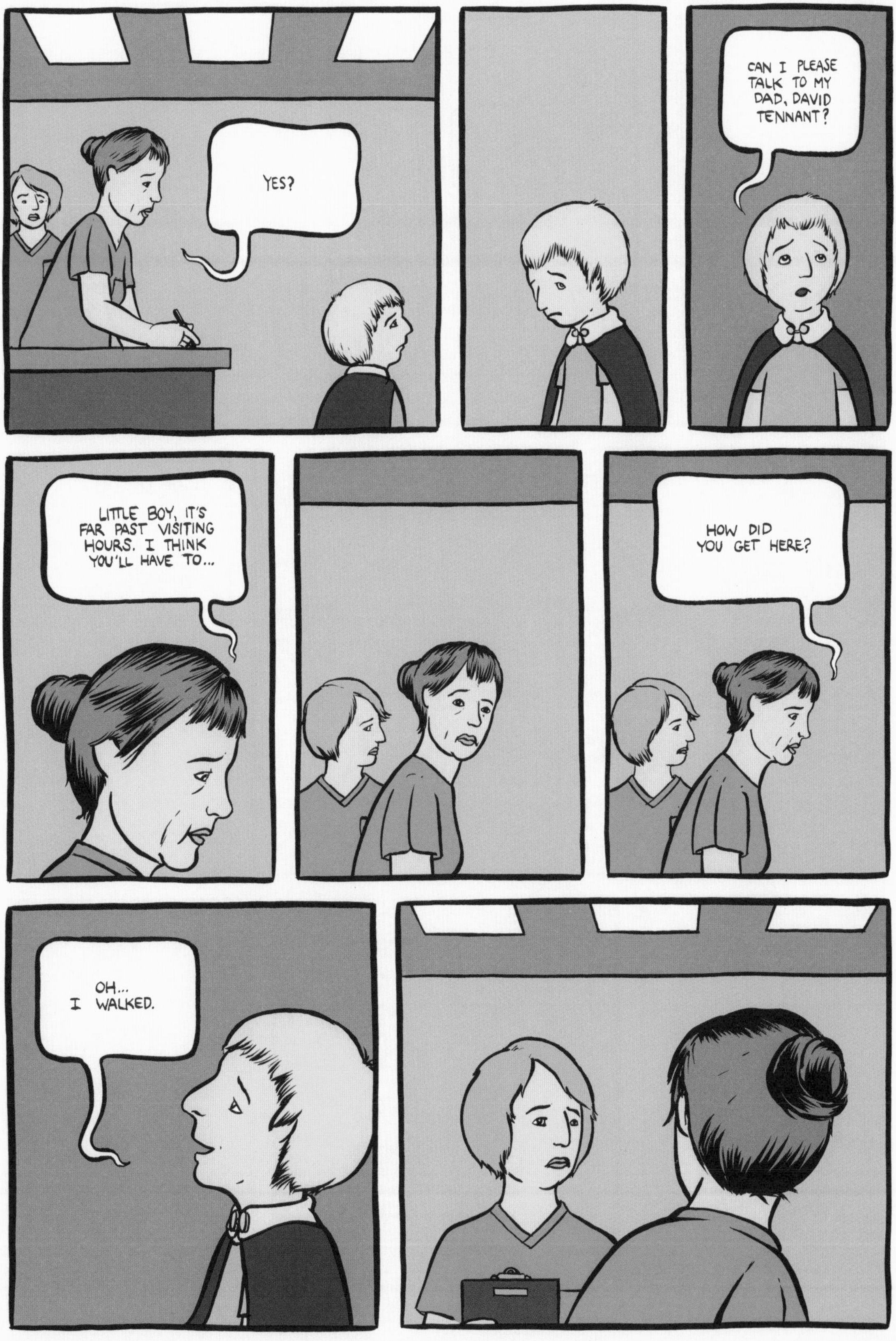
YES?
CAN I PLEASE TALK TO MY DAD, DAVID TENNANT?
LITTLE BOY, IT'S FAR PAST VISITING HOURS. I THINK YOU'LL HAVE TO...
HOW DID YOU GET HERE?
OH... I WALKED.

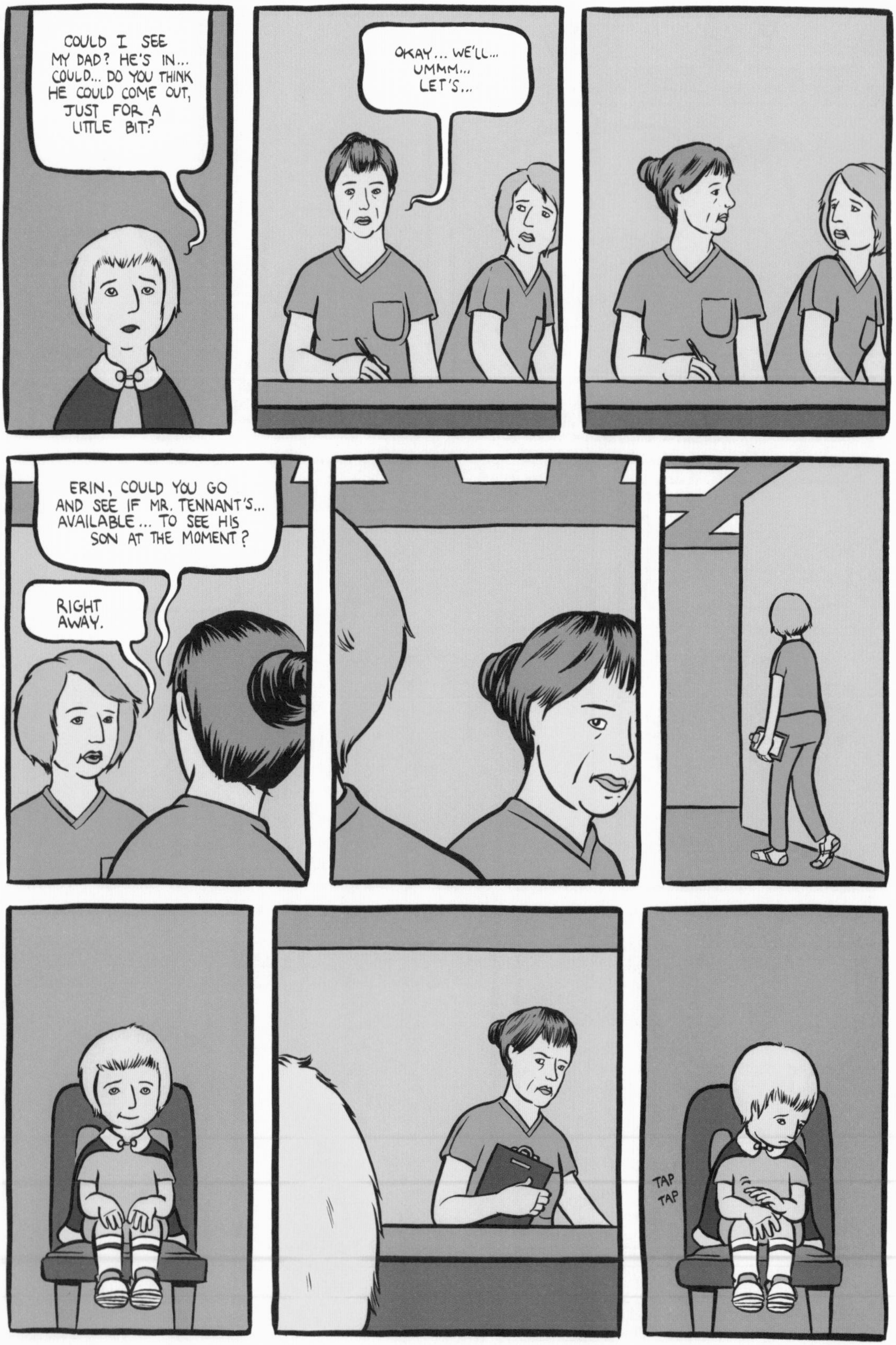
COULD I SEE MY DAD? HE'S IN... COULD... DO YOU THINK HE COULD COME OUT, JUST FOR A LITTLE BIT?
OKAY... WE'LL... UMMM... LET'S...
ERIN, COULD YOU GO AND SEE IF MR. TENNANT'S... AVAILABLE... TO SEE HIS SON AT THE MOMENT?
RIGHT AWAY.
TAP TAP

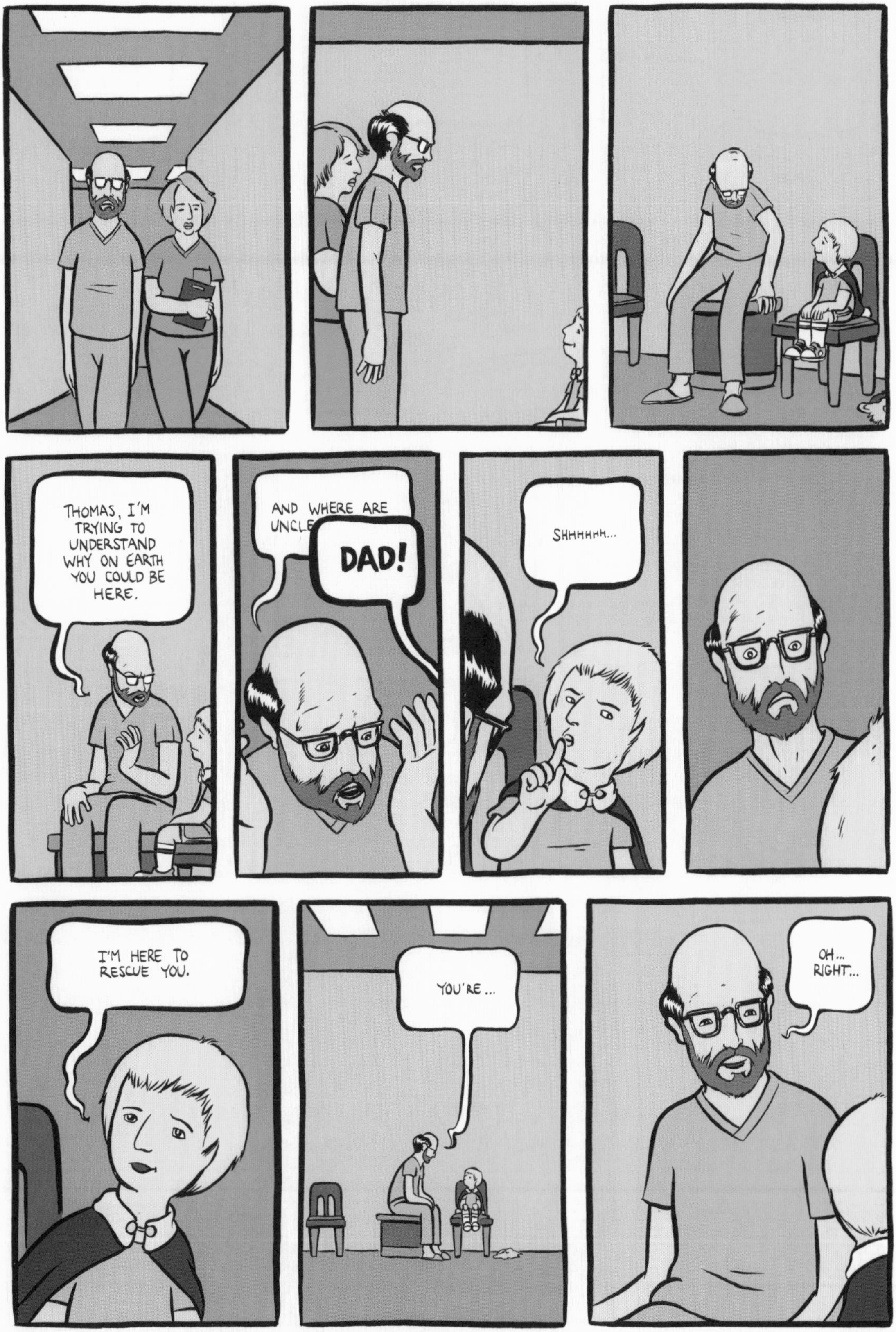
THOMAS, I'M TRYING TO UNDERSTAND WHY ON EARTH YOU COULD BE HERE.
AND WHERE ARE UNCLE
DAD!
SHHHHHH...
I'M HERE TO RESCUE YOU.
YOU'RE...
OH... RIGHT...

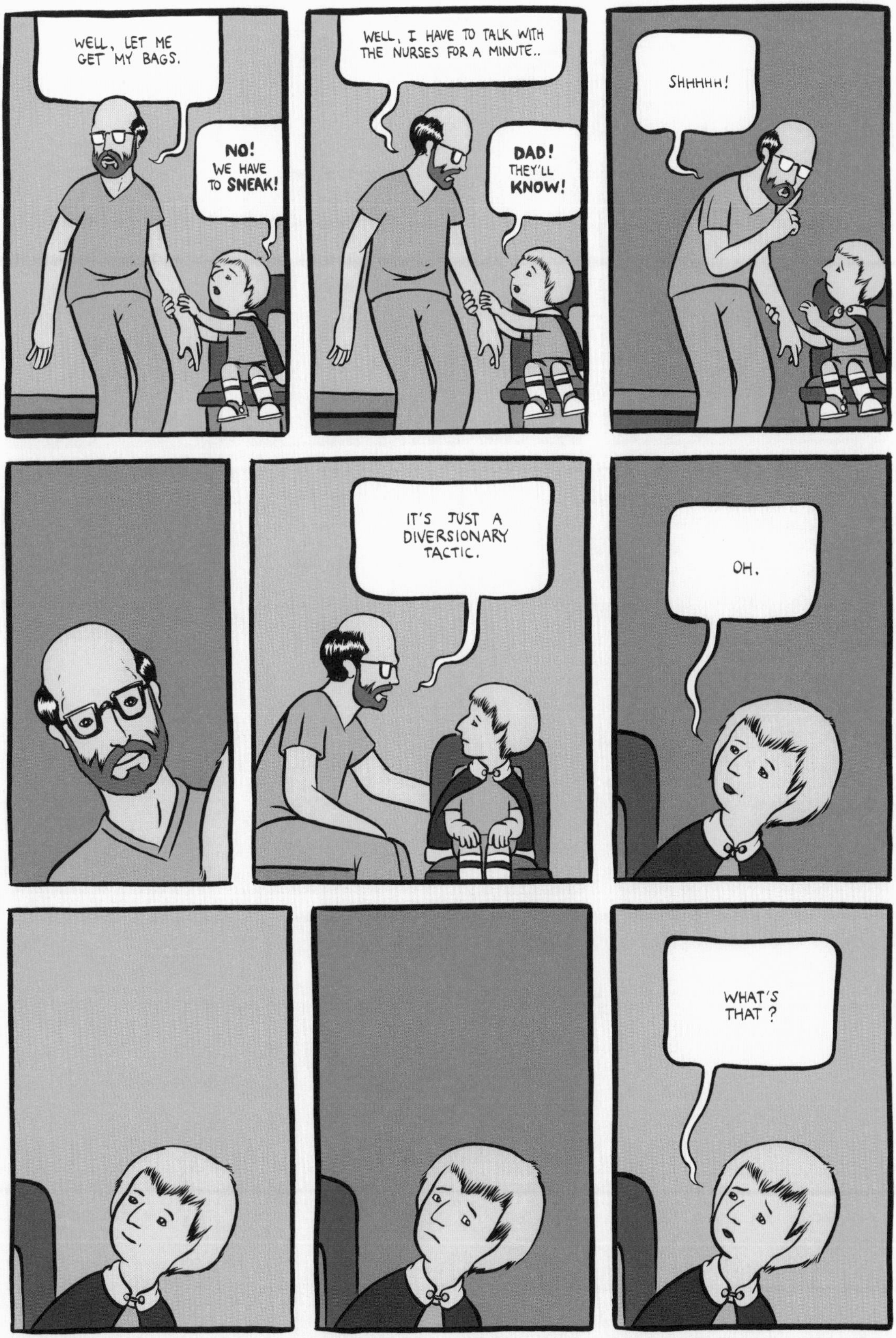
WELL, LET ME GET MY BAGS.
NO! WE HAVE TO SNEAK!
WELL, I HAVE TO TALK WITH THE NURSES FOR A MINUTE..
DAD! THEY'LL KNOW!
SHHHHH!
IT'S JUST A DIVERSIONARY TACTIC.
OH.
WHAT'S THAT ?

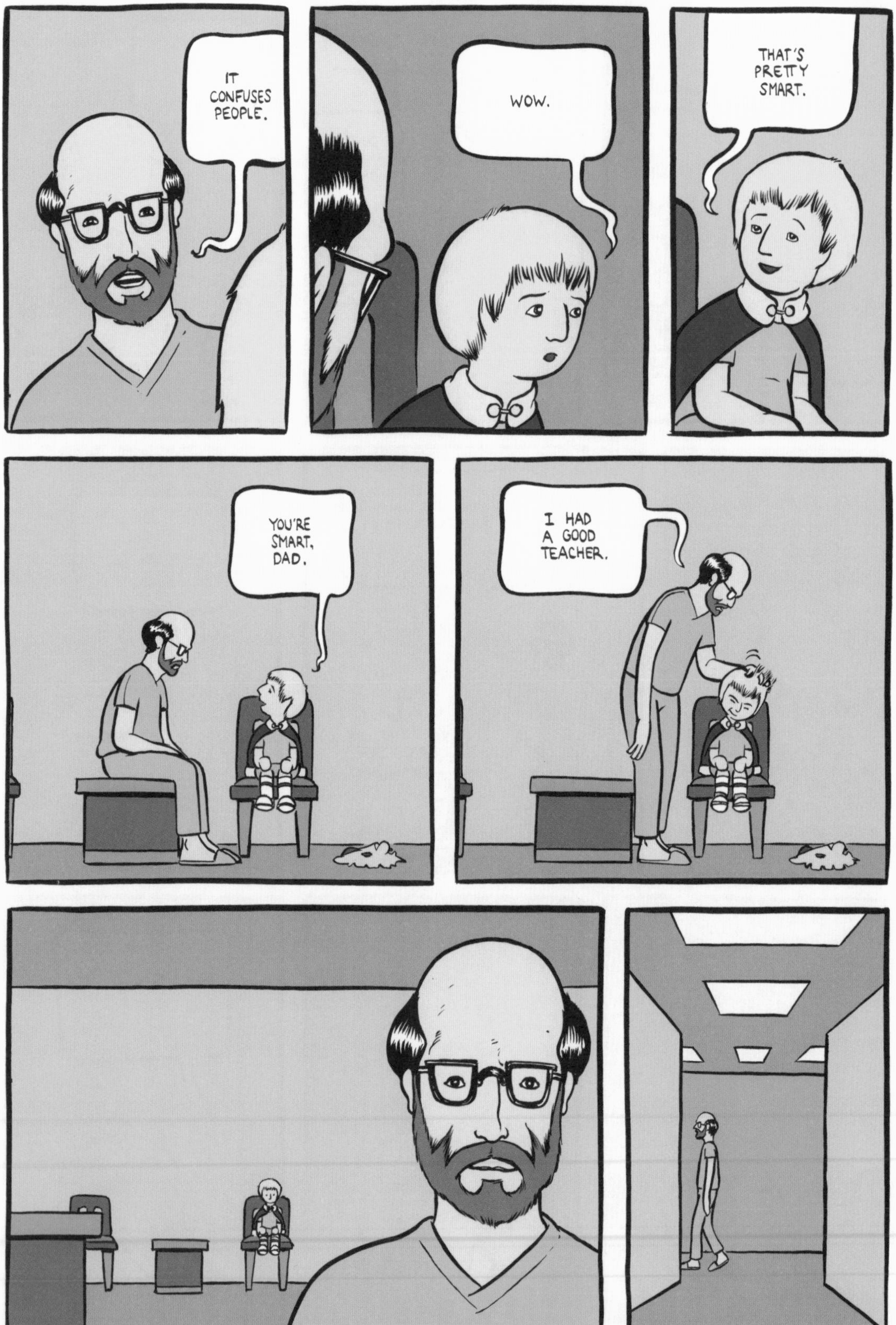
IT CONFUSES PEOPLE.
WOW.
THAT'S PRETTY SMART.
YOU'RE SMART, DAD.
I HAD A GOOD TEACHER.

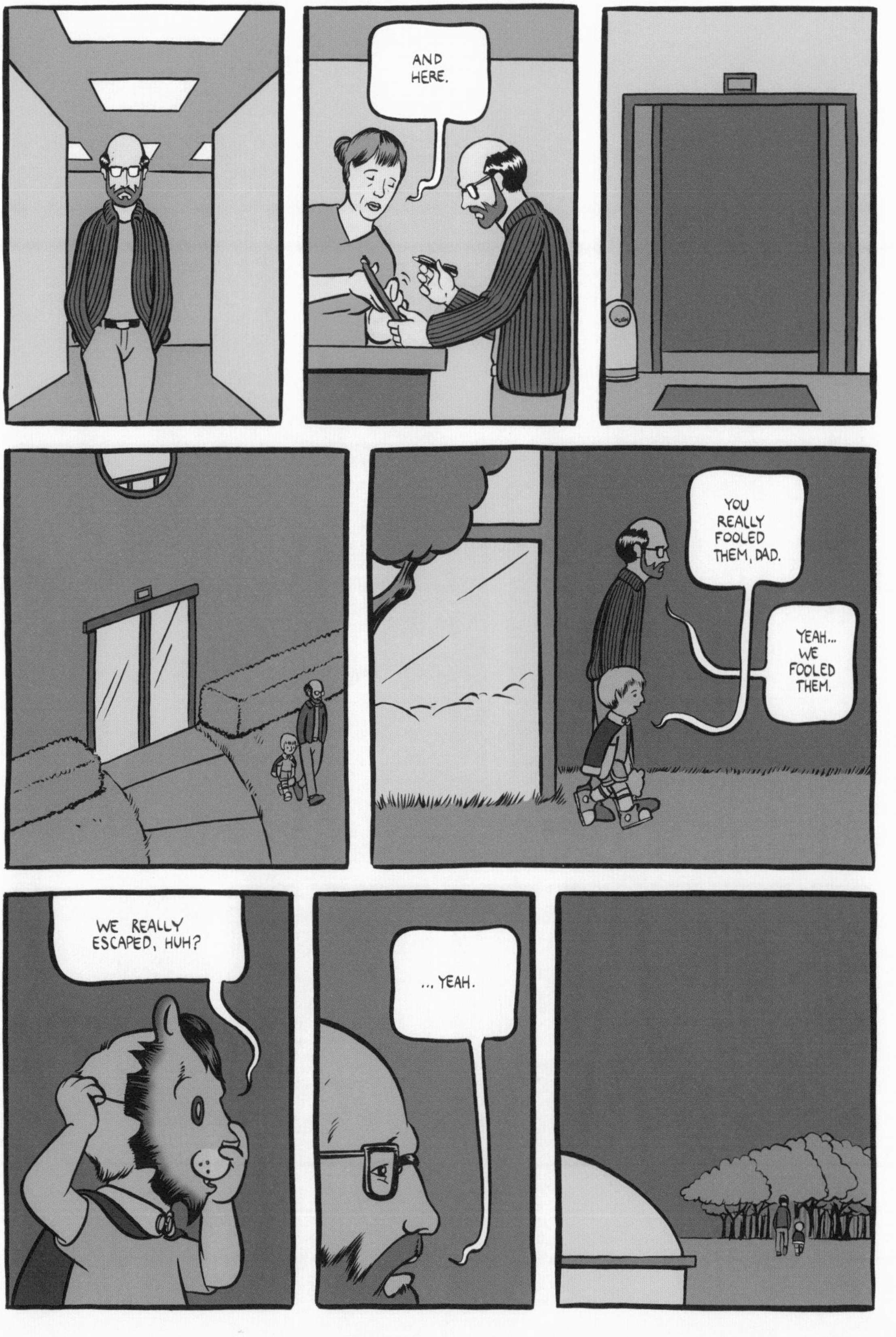
AND HERE.
YOU REALLY FOOLED THEM, DAD.
YEAH... WE FOOLED THEM.
WE REALLY ESCAPED, HUH?
... YEAH.

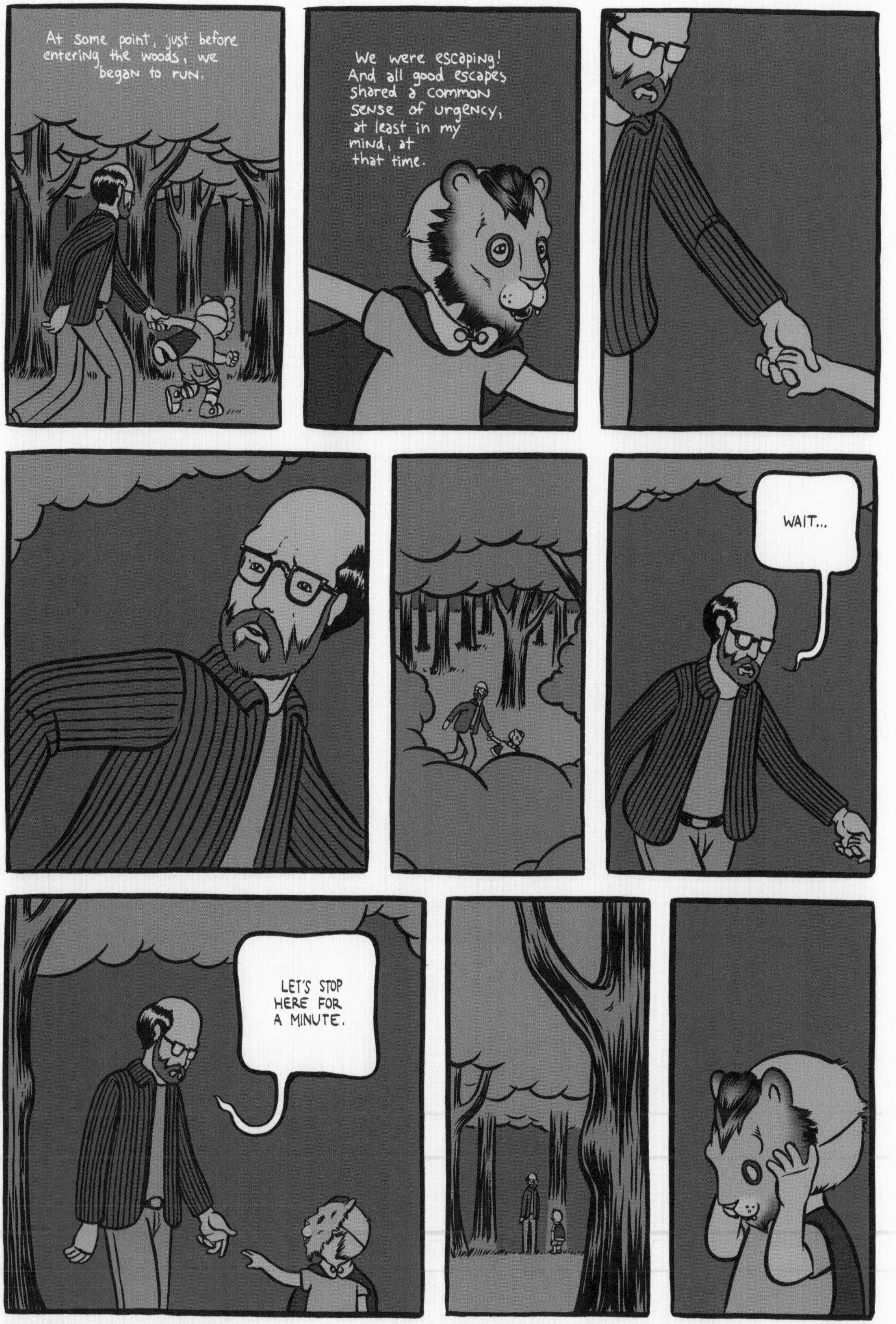
At some point, just before entering the woods, we began to run.
We were escaping! And all good escapes shared a common sense of urgency, at least in my mind, at that time.
WAIT...
LET'S STOP HERE FOR A MINUTE.

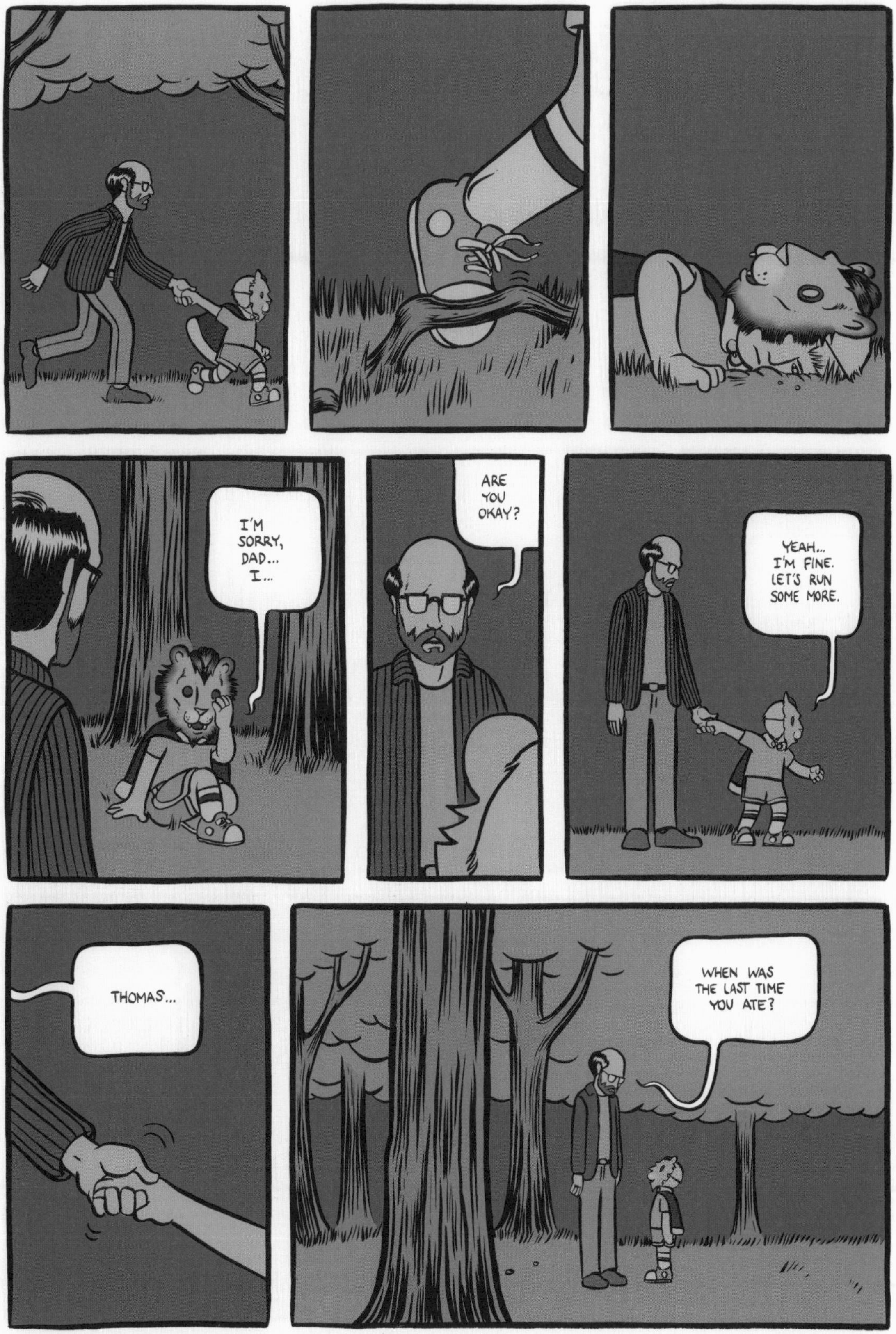
I'M SORRY, DAD... I...
ARE YOU OKAY?
YEAH... I'M FINE. LET'S RUN SOME MORE.
THOMAS...
WHEN WAS THE LAST TIME YOU ATE?

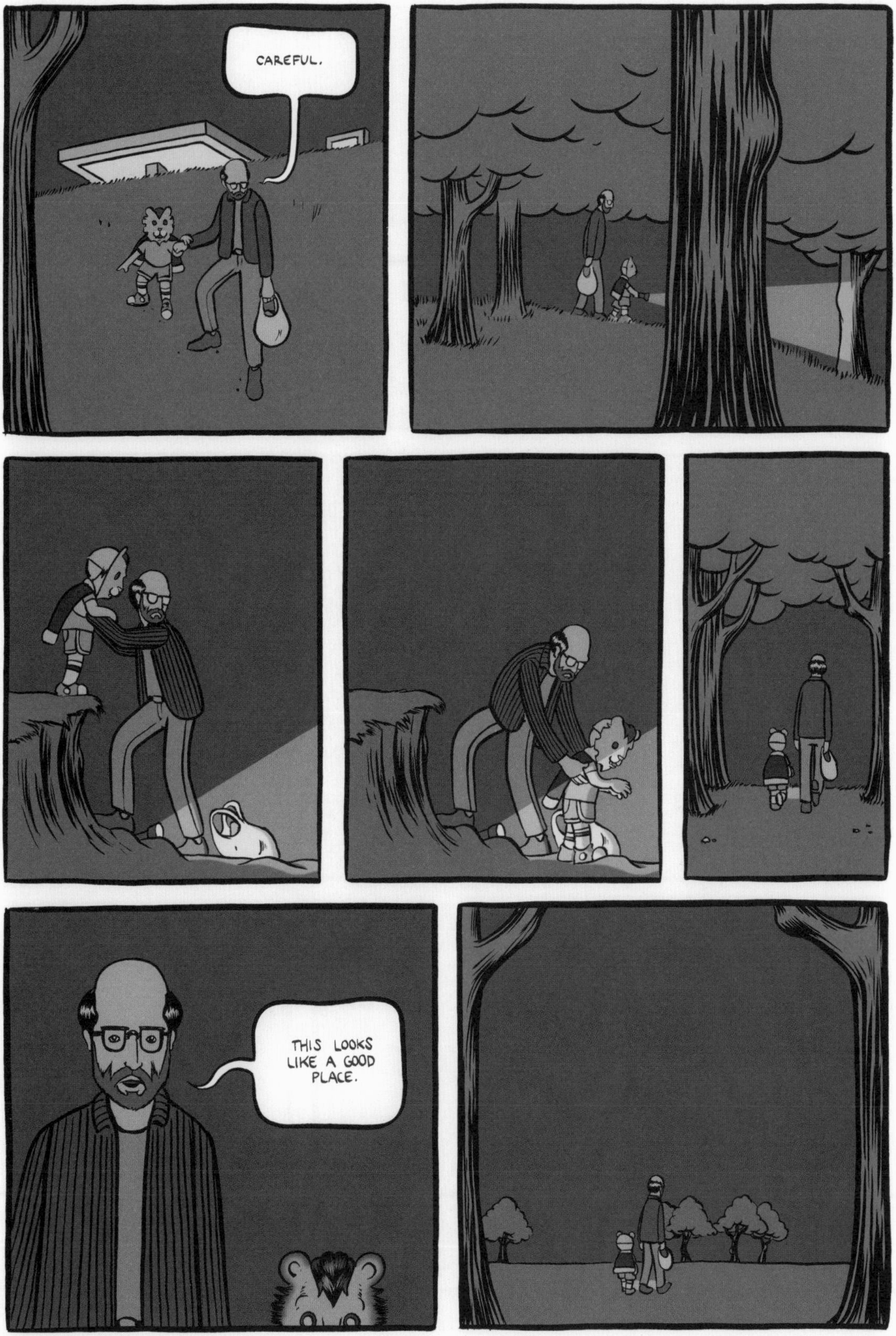
CAREFUL.
THIS LOOKS LIKE A GOOD PLACE.

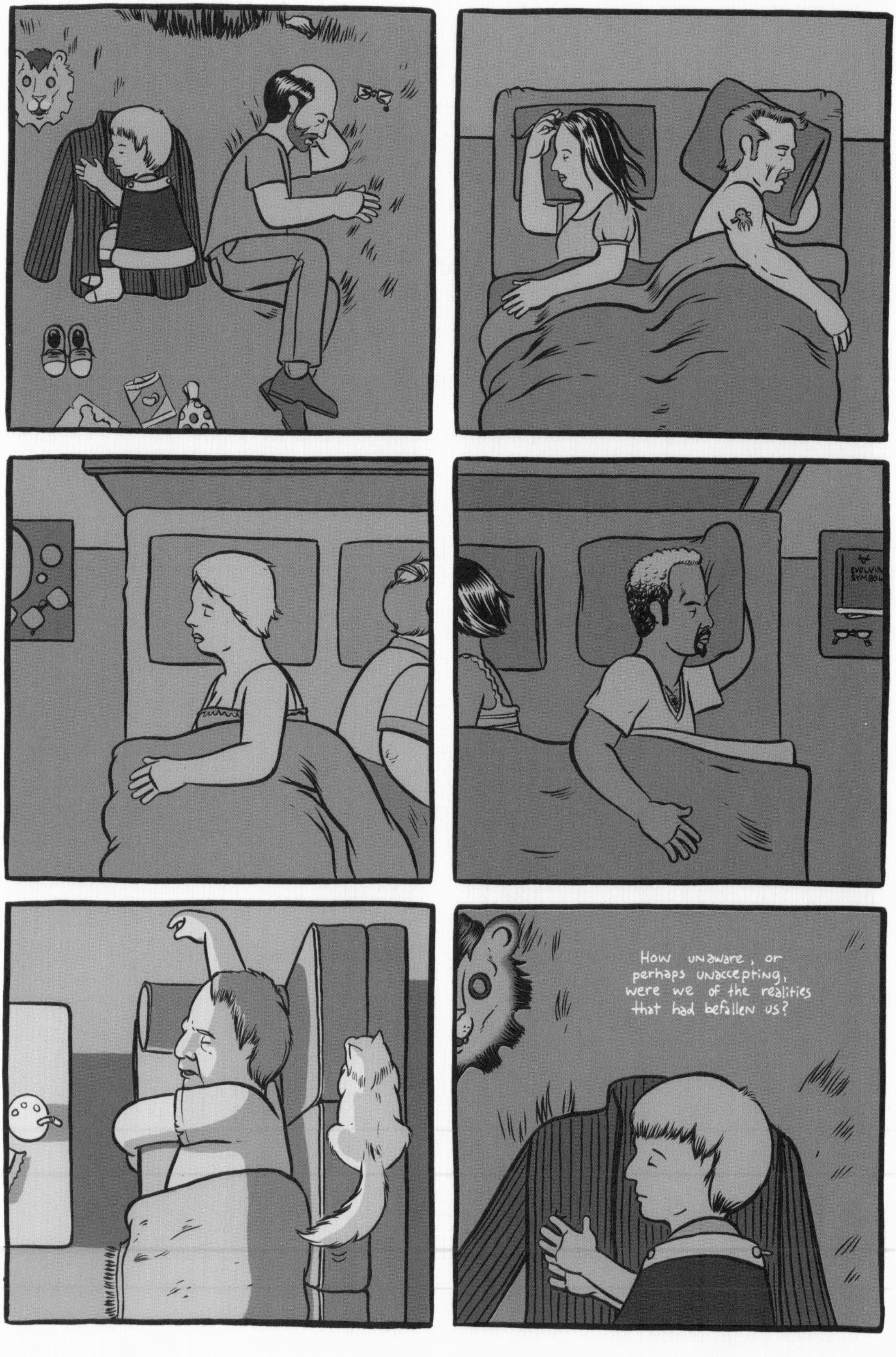
How unaware, or perhaps unaccepting, were we of the realities that had befallen us?

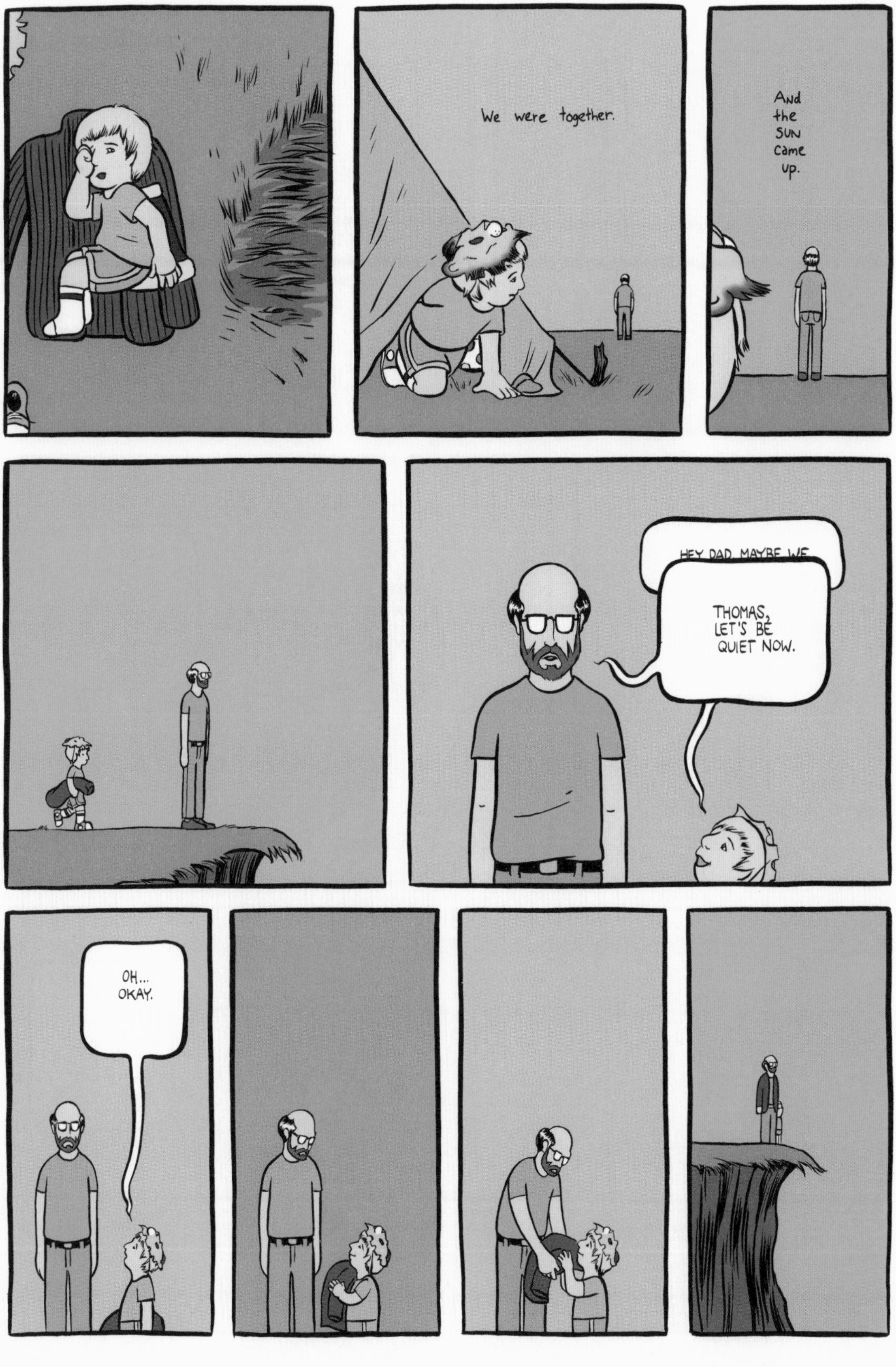
We were together.
And the sun came up.
HEY DAD, MAYBE WE
THOMAS, LET'S BE QUIET NOW.
OH... OKAY.

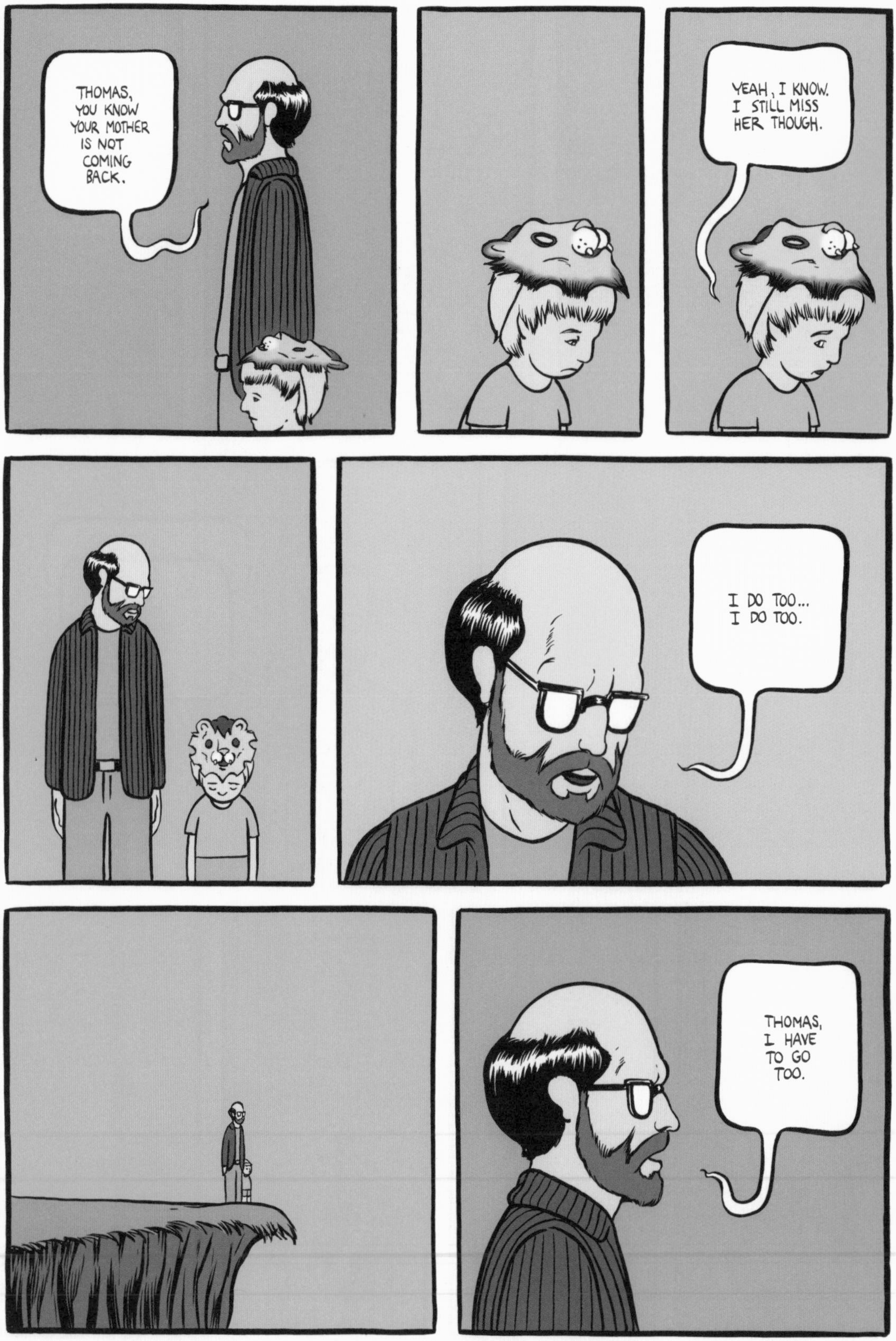
THOMAS, YOU KNOW YOUR MOTHER IS NOT COMING BACK.
YEAH, I KNOW. I STILL MISS HER THOUGH.
I DO TOO... I DO TOO.
THOMAS, I HAVE TO GO TOO.

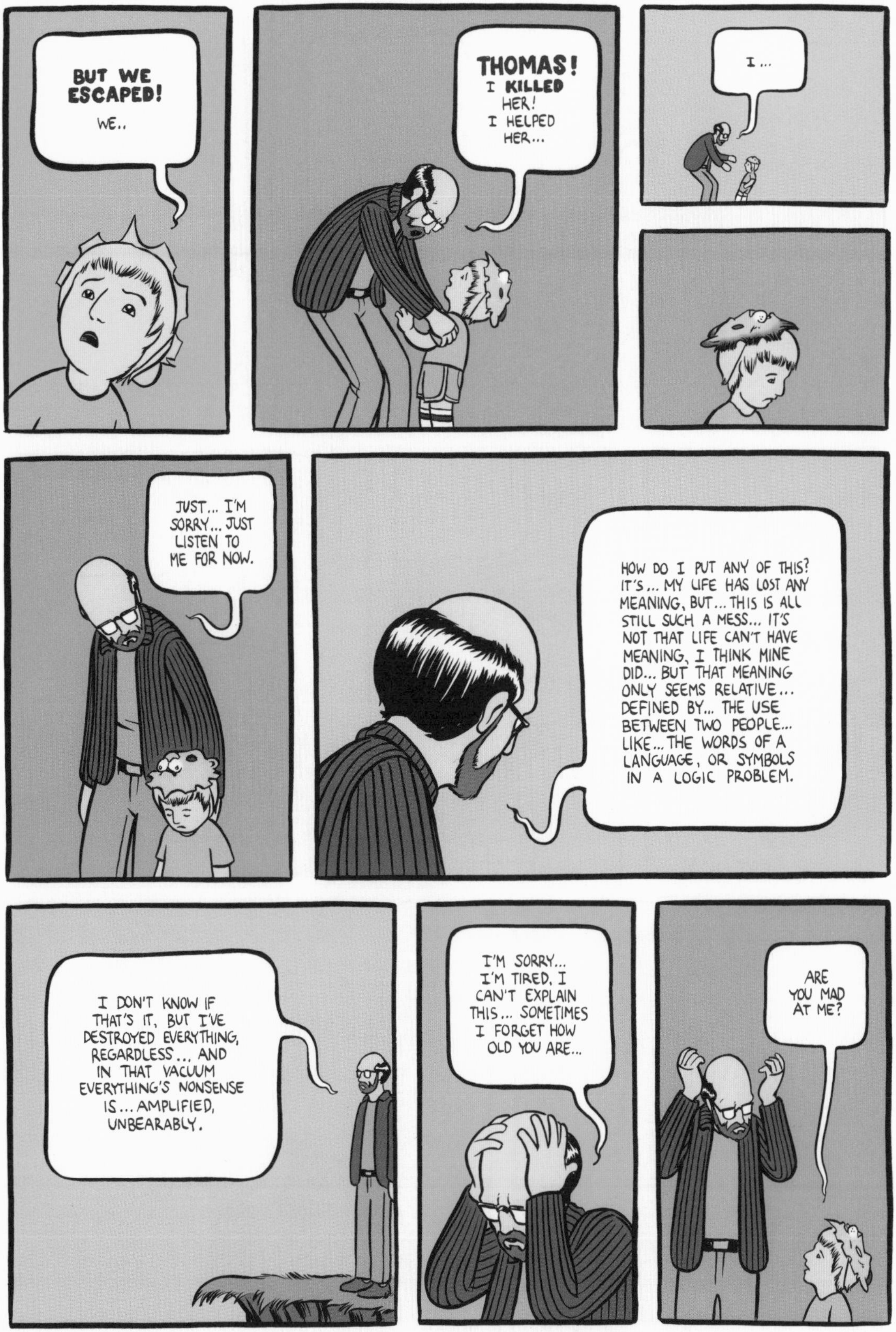
BUT WE ESCAPED! WE..
THOMAS! I KILLED HER! I HELPED HER...
I...
JUST... I'M SORRY... JUST LISTEN TO ME FOR NOW.
HOW DO I PUT ANY OF THIS? IT'S... MY LIFE HAS LOST ANY MEANING, BUT... THIS IS ALL STILL SUCH A MESS... IT'S NOT THAT LIFE CAN'T HAVE MEANING, I THINK MINE DID... BUT THAT MEANING ONLY SEEMS RELATIVE... DEFINED BY... THE USE BETWEEN TWO PEOPLE... LIKE... THE WORDS OF A LANGUAGE, OR SYMBOLS IN A LOGIC PROBLEM.
I DON'T KNOW IF THAT'S IT, BUT I'VE DESTROYED EVERYTHING, REGARDLESS... AND IN THAT VACUUM EVERYTHING'S NONSENSE IS... AMPLIFIED, UNBEARABLY.
I'M SORRY... I'M TIRED, I CAN'T EXPLAIN THIS... SOMETIMES I FORGET HOW OLD YOU ARE...
ARE YOU MAD AT ME?

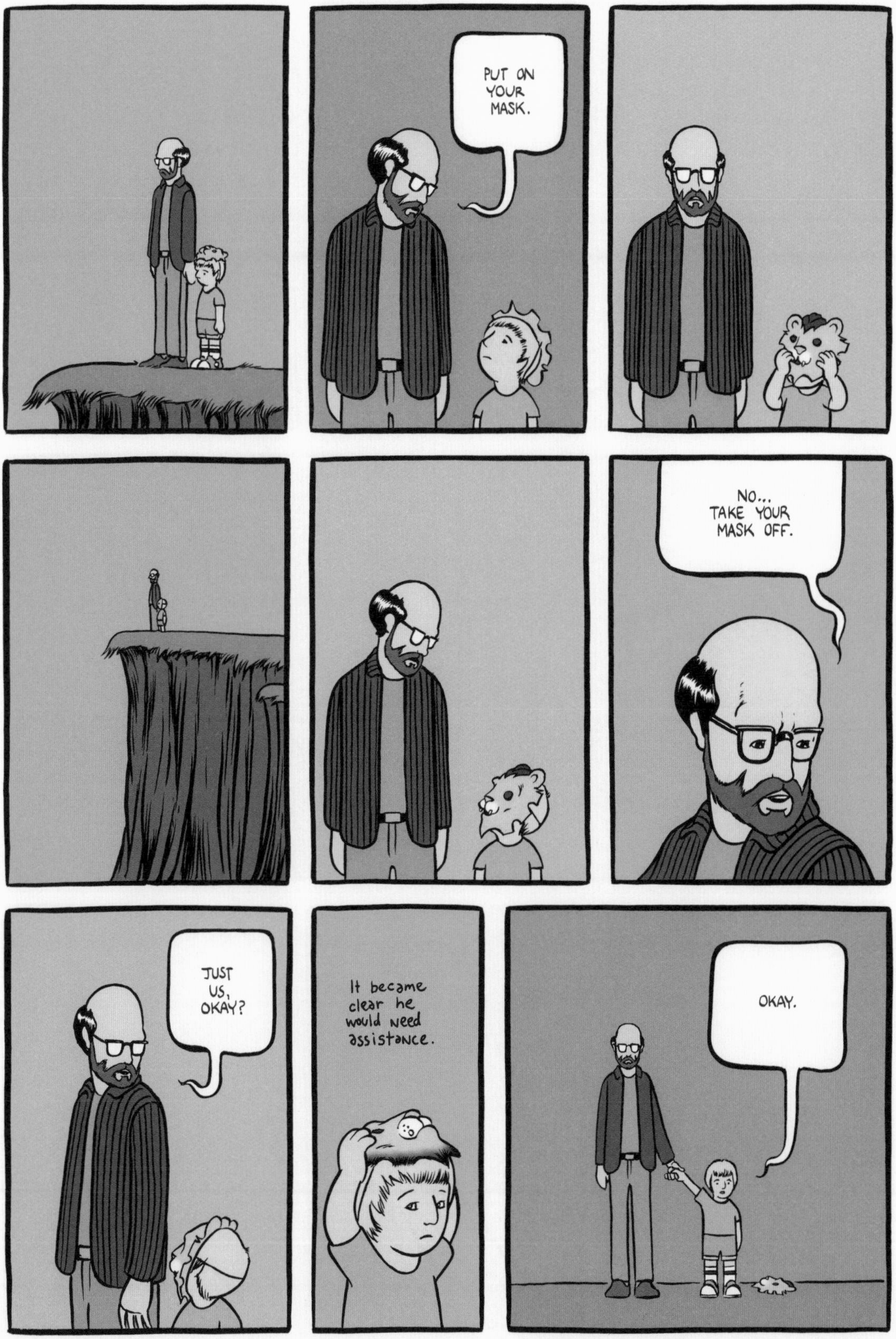
PUT ON YOUR MASK.
NO... TAKE YOUR MASK OFF.
JUST US, OKAY?
It became clear he would need assistance.
OKAY.

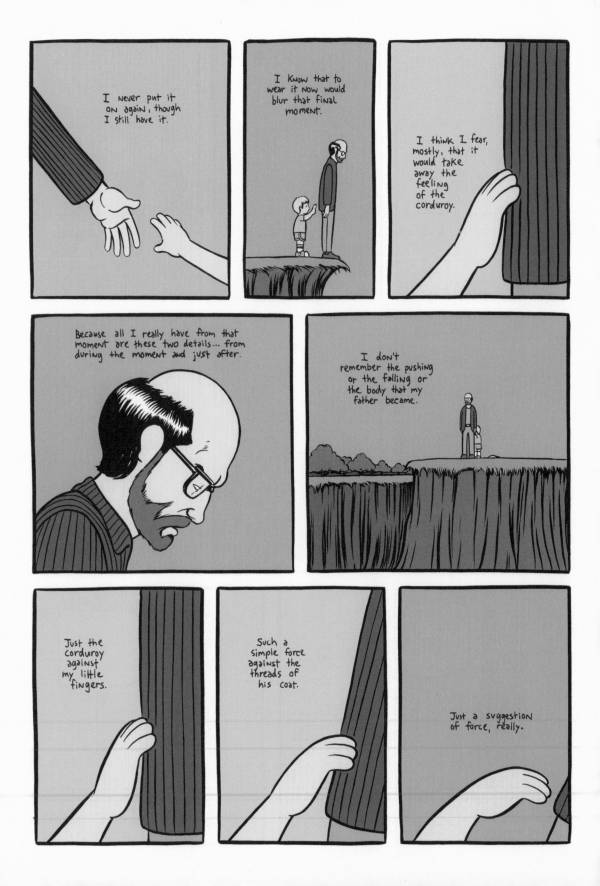

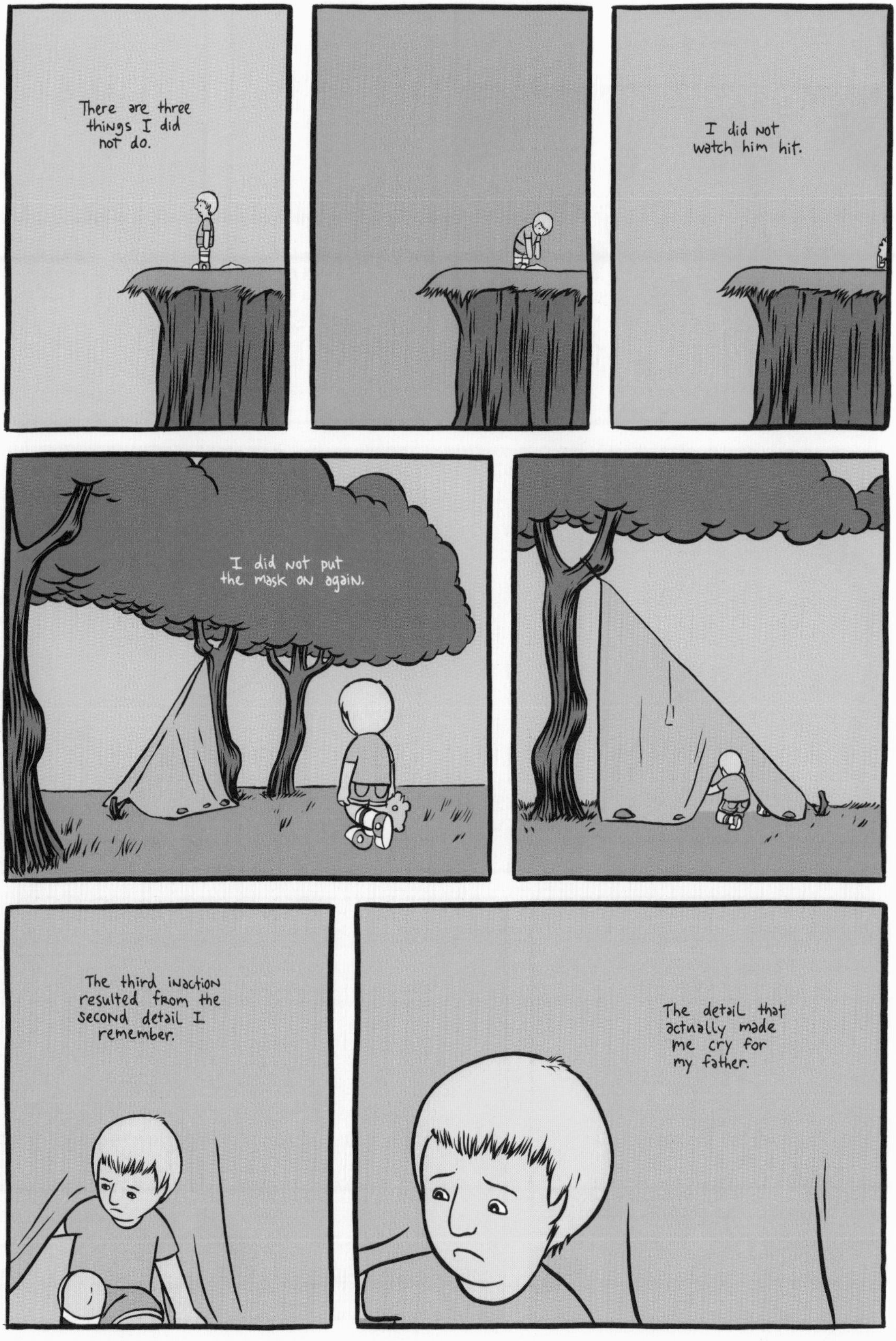
There are three things I did not do.
I did not watch him hit.
I did not put the mask on again.
The third inaction resulted from the second detail I remember.
The detail that actually made me cry for my father.

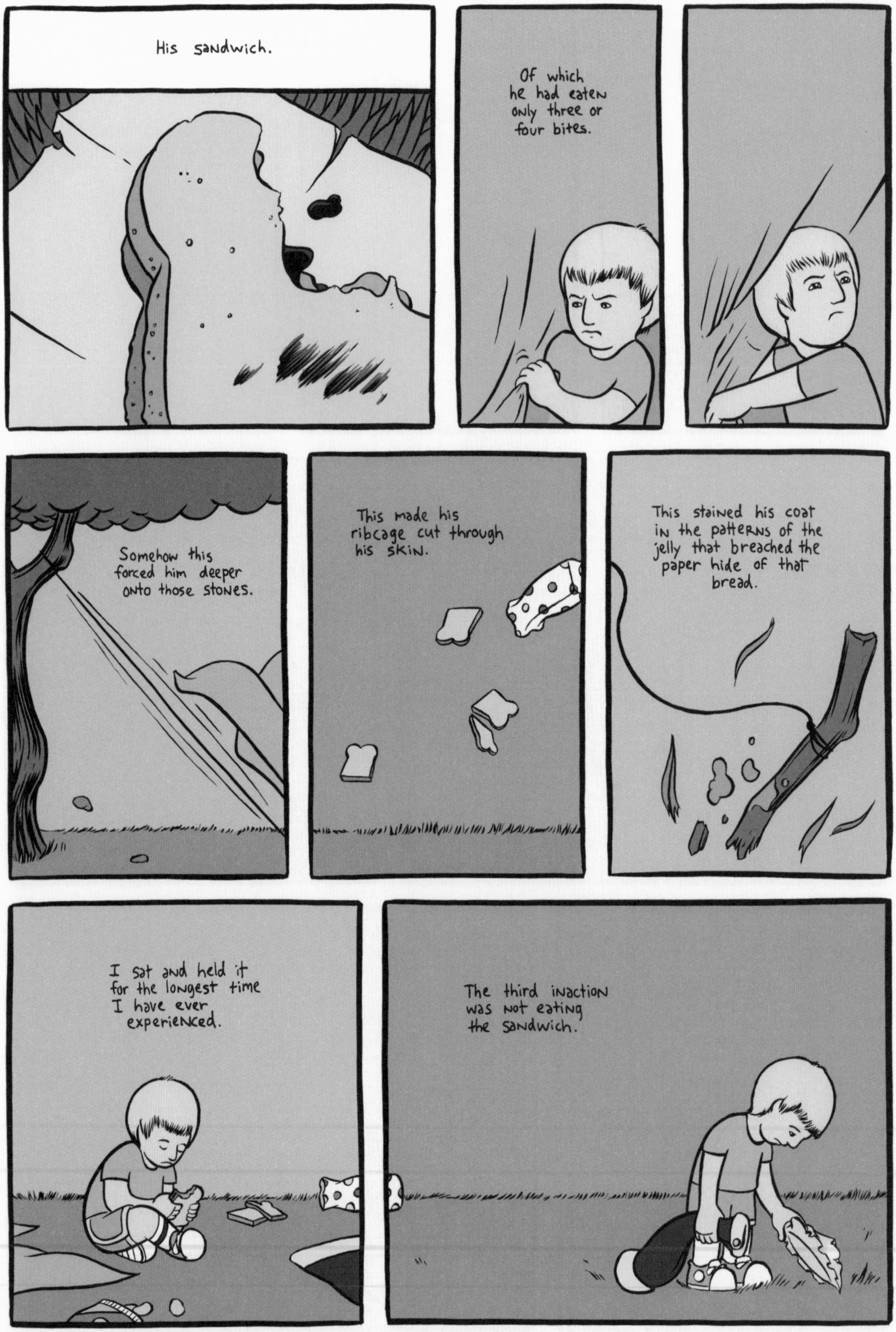
His sandwich.
Of which he had eaten only three or four bites.
Somehow this forced him deeper onto those stones.
This made his ribcage cut through his skin.
This stained his coat in the patterns of the jelly that breached the paper hide of that bread.
I sat and held it for the longest time I have ever experienced.
The third inaction was not eating the sandwich.

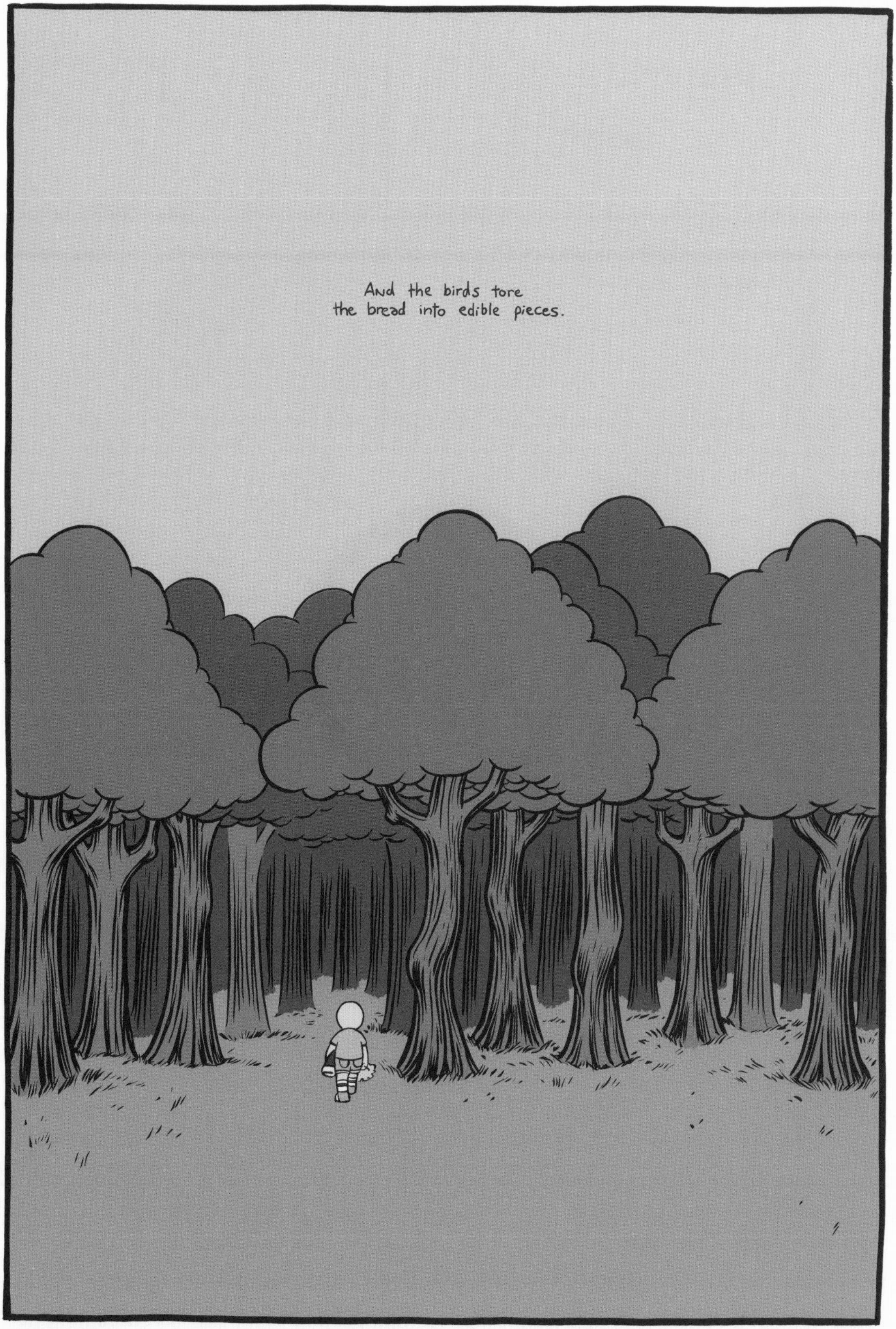
And the birds tore the bread into edible pieces.

END OF INTRODUCTION

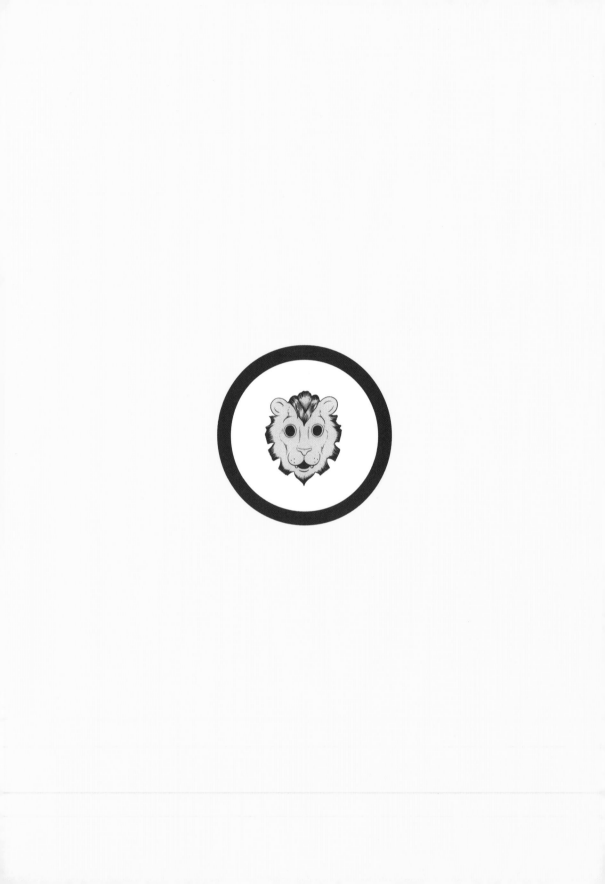

CHAPTER ONE

"WE ARE ALL RELEASED"

Many Thanks

There are many who have suffered needlessly, or given generously, or some combination thereof, during the production of this book. They are thanked here, inadequately, by listing their names: Patrick Hornschemeier, Margaret Clark, Ann and Mary Hornschemeier, Diana Schutz, Ed Irvin, Kathleen Kranack, Professor Neil Tennant, Josh Farkas, Jeffrey Brown, Anders Nilsen, John Hankiewicz, Bo Altes, Mat Biscan, Dan Hyatt, Lisa Jaronski, Chelsea Bauer-Greene, Farel Dalrymple, Chris Young, Will Eisner, Frank Miller, Craig Thompson, Nick Bertozzi, Chris Ware, Dan Raeburn, Erynn Wheatley, Michelle Patterson, Dwight Dyer, Sammy Harkham, Chris Pitzer, Brett Warnock, Tomer Hanuka, Tom Herpich, James Jean, Richard Hahn, Eric Cardiff, Kelli Flanery, Daniel Bishop, Cheryl Weaver, Jay Ryan, Postergirl Press, Henry Owings, Quimby's Bookstore, all cartoonists whose conversations helped urge this collection forward, and all readers and letter writers who made the pursuit worthwhile. And immeasurable thanks to Tchaikovsky and Sigur Ros, to whose music most of this collection was drawn.

Original art from this and other works by the author are available through:
www.beguiling.com
www.comicartcollective.com

Books, prints, and other materials are available from:

www.theholyconsumption.com

Or to contact the author :
thomas@forlornfunnies.com

About The Author

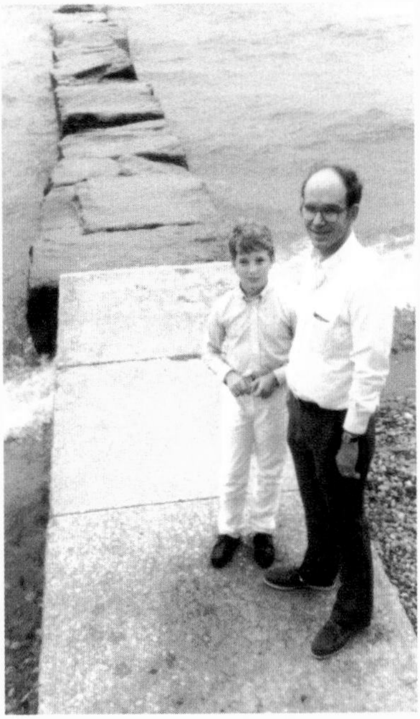

PAUL HORNSCHEMEIER was born in Cincinnati in 1977 and was reared in rural Georgetown, Ohio. While attending college, he began to publish his experimental comics series, *Sequential*. He currently resides in Chicago with his cat Margo, while producing his regular series, *Forlorn Funnies*, which has garnered Ignatz, Eisner, and Harvey nominations.

GALLERY

PROMOTIONAL ARTWORK
FROM THE FIRST EDITION

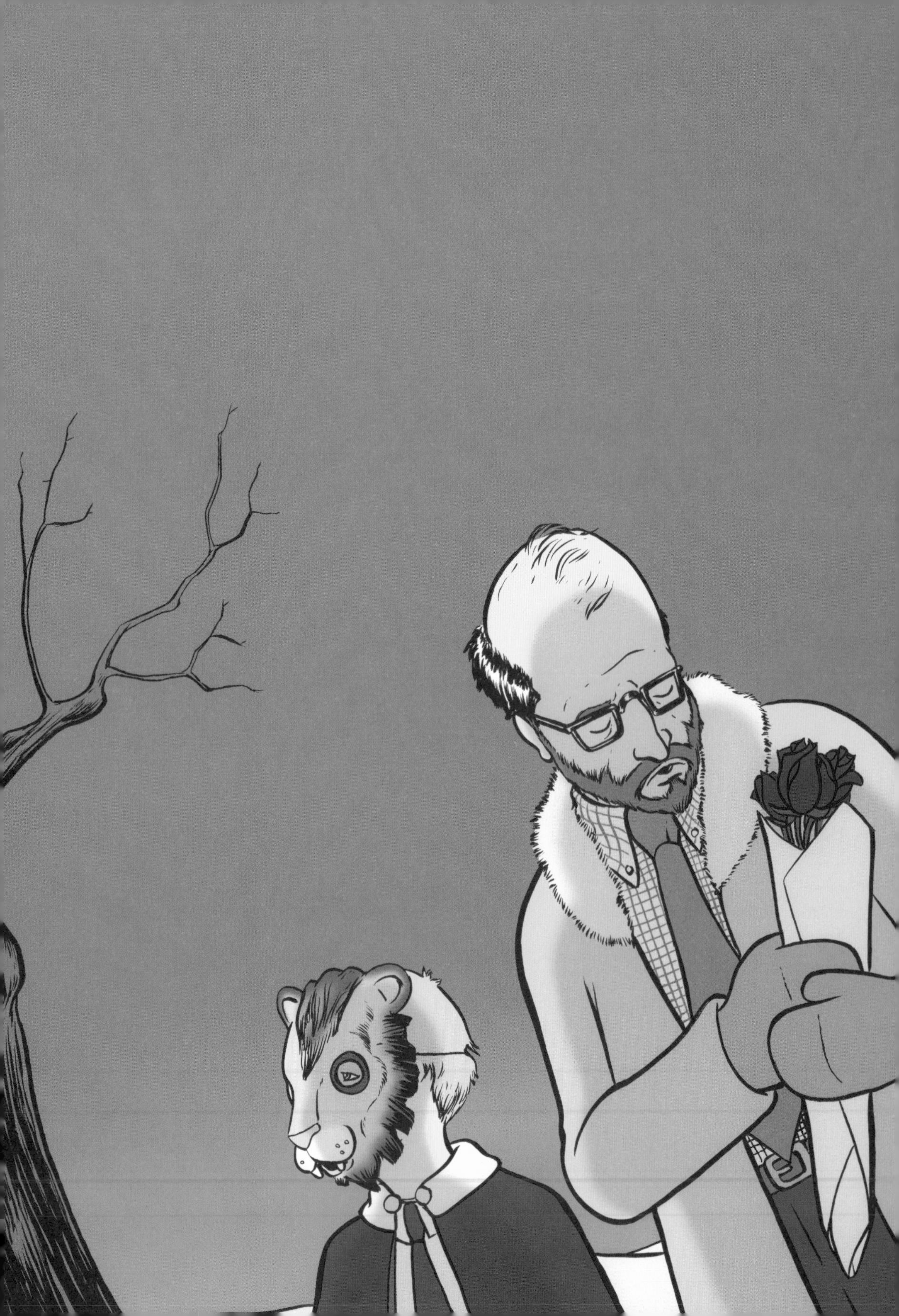

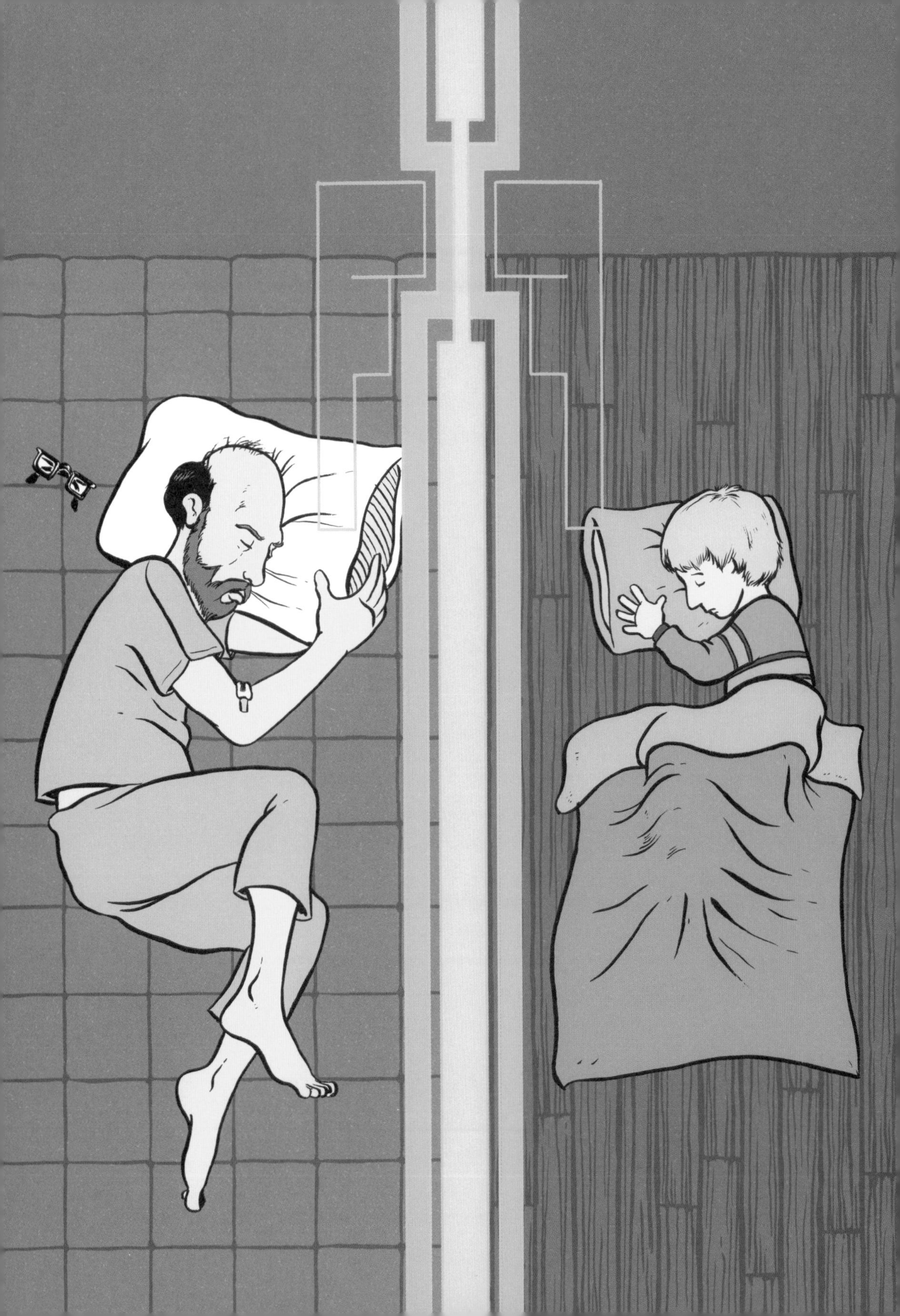

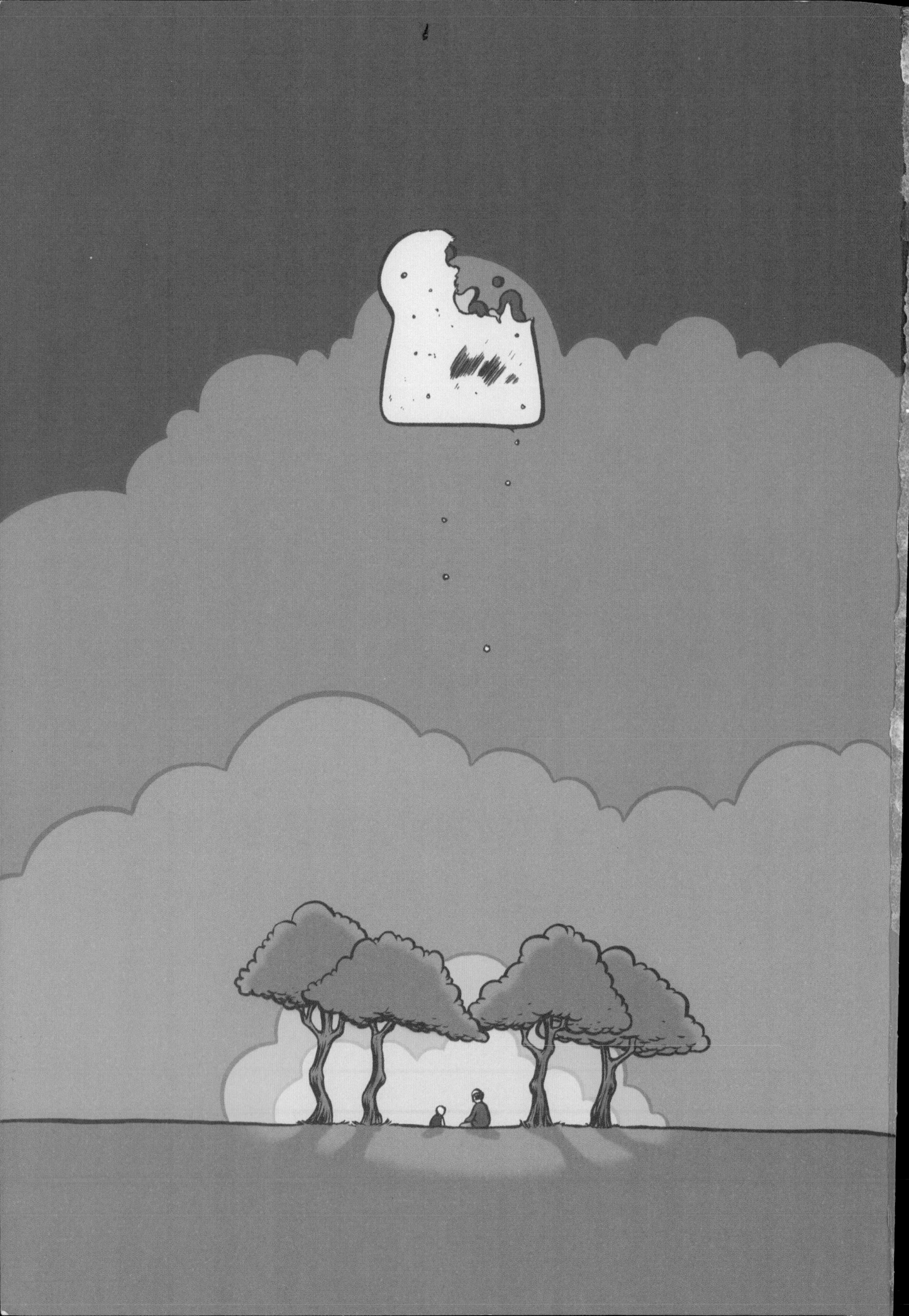